FROM VICTIM
TO VIRTUOUS

FROM VICTIM TO VIRTUOUS

*A JOURNEY AND BLUEPRINT TO BECOMING A VIRTUOUS WOMAN...***FOR ALL WOMEN FROM THE POOREST NEIGHBORHOODS TO HOLLYWOOD**

With Journal

YOLANDA MARSHALL

Copyright © 2010 by Yolanda Marshall

Glimpse of Glory Christian Book Publishing
459 Main Street, Suite 101-125
Trussville, AL 35173

Unless otherwise noted Scriptures are taken from King James Version Bible.

All rights reserved. No part of this publication may be reproduced, stored in a retrieval system or transmitted, in any form, or by any means, electronic, mechanical, recorded, photocopied, or otherwise, without the prior permission of the copyright owner, except by a reviewer who may quote brief passages in a review.

ISBN: 978-0-578-04366-1

Printed in the United States of America

CONTENTS

FROM VICTIM TO VIRTUOUS 7
THE VIRTUOUS WOMAN 11
ACKNOWLEDGEMENT 13
FOREWORD 17
PREFACE 19
INTRODUCTION 21
PART ONE 25
PART TWO 33
PART THREE 47
CHAPTER 1: A ROADMAP TO VIRTUE...
CRACKING THE SHELL TO BREAK THE YOKE 81
CHAPTER 2: AMOROUS 97
CHAPTER 3: VIGILANT 105
CHAPTER 4: INTERCESSOR 114
CHAPTER 5: RIGHTEOUS 120
CHAPTER 6: TRUTHFUL 129
CHAPTER 7: UNDERSTANDING 136
CHAPTER 8: OBEDIENT 147
CHAPTER 9: UNCOMPROMISING 154
CHAPTER 10: SENSITIVE 158
CHAPTER 11: WISE 169
CHAPTER 12: OVERCOMER 174
CHAPTER 13: MEEK 181
CHAPTER 14: ATTENTIVE 199
CHAPTER 15: NURTURING 203

BONUS NOTE 210
WORDS OF ENCOURAGEMENT 212
A PRAYER FOR WOMEN 213
SCRIPTURE READINGS 215
ABOUT THE AUTHOR 218

From Victim To Virtuous

EACH of us has been victims of common circumstances in our lives. When I think about the negative cycles many of us have repeated, I clearly understand the true essence of our actions. As I look back, I find myself questioning why we made the decisions in the first place to move in an unhealthy direction. Paradoxically, our decisions have obviously moved us from maintaining an emotional, mental, social, physical, and spiritual balance. We are victims of brokenness.

This alone is a disease that spreads beyond measure just as cancer spreads to other areas of our lives and further damages us. This has caused us to become victims of alcohol, drugs, low self-esteem, selfishness, jealousy, anger, compulsion…multi-faceted abuses from others and ourselves, and the list goes on. I was once a victim of brokenness, which adversely affected other areas of my life— but God, delivered me!

It is my desire that upon reading *From Victim to Virtuous*, you will claim and receive the position God has intended for you as well to become—A Virtuous Woman. As your desire for wholeness propels you toward a healthier and happier you, it is then that you will discover a special strength to embrace this season in which you now find yourself full with hope, faith, and confidence.

There is a gap that exists between living life as a victim and one of virtue—and it is within this void that discovery, recovery, healing, deliverance, and freedom bridges the gap between victim and virtuous. Believe me! This is a good place to be in your life, so embrace the moment and receive the truth.

The following process is needed for you to close the gap and lead to new experiences with you at the helm as a victor:

1) Discovery: You can actually identify the root cause of your bro-

kenness and where it stems from in this process of your life. To work toward solving any problem, you must first recognize that a "problem" exists. After locating this problem you can then advance to the next level. I used the three-fold confession method, which moved me toward wholeness. First, you must be honest with yourself [recognize there is a problem]. Secondly, you must be honest with God [tell Him about all of your problems]. Lastly, you must be honest with others [many can tell you have a problem before you ever mention it to them anyway].

It is this disease [brokenness] that has caused a growth block in many women's lives—the overall growth necessary [in order] to fulfill your ultimate purpose. Seemingly, when you find yourself repeating negative cycles over and over again, the adverse circumstances should compel you to self-examine every part of your life. By doing so, you may find that what happened between your childhood and adulthood has had an impact on your thought processes, which play a major part in your continuing to repeat these negative cycles. In speaking with several women and even studying women through observation and conversation, I have learned that a lot of issues we have today stem from our childhood. What happened?

2) Recovery: You will be able to reclaim your true identity in this process of your life—the identity that God gave you even before you entered your mother's womb. In Jeremiah 1:5 we read, "Before I formed thee in the belly I knew thee; and before thou camest forth out of the womb I sanctified thee, and I ordained thee a prophet unto the nations." A Virtuous Woman! In order to move forward, you must be restored. Restoration is a pivotal point in your growth. This is a time that needs to be celebrated with self-love and pampering, and above all, you must practice "patience." We must love ourselves enough to realize the importance of recovery and be patient enough with ourselves to ensure full recovery and put an end to the choice to continue being a victim of brokenness. Many have claimed other statuses

because of our brokenness. This is contrary to whom God says you are—statuses the world has given you. In reclaiming your identity, you should partner with God to seek His help in sustaining you, even at times when you do not think you are worthy.

3) Healing: Your wounds of brokenness are sealed in this process of your life. Since you have discovered the root cause of this disease called brokenness, and you have used the three-fold confession method, and you are now in recovery, you can get ready to receive your total healing—Now. You can expect to be healed from repeating these negatives cycles, namely bad relationships. This is seemingly the most common cycle many women have repeated, and it is this kind of cycle that breaks us even further.

4) Deliverance: You can really experience the mighty hand of God move on your behalf in this process of your life. You are on the road of deliverance. After partnering with Him, you can expect the power, along with constant prayer, faith, and action to break the shackles of brokenness. In Exodus 6:6, God told Moses to tell the children of Israel, "I am the Lord, and I will bring you out from under the burdens of the Egyptians, and I will rid you out of their bondage, and I will redeem you with a stretched out arm, and with great judgment. God wants to deliver you *NOW*. Once you are delivered, do not expect to return to where you were delivered. You are no longer affected, no matter who says you are—you are set free!

5) Freedom: You can make better sense of who you really are, without the hindrances of being a broken person in this process of your life. You are released and you are whole. You can now live the healthy and happy life you have desired and fulfill your destiny. You must remember that you were born with a purpose. There is nothing greater than experiencing a life of freedom to build a solid relationship with God, and to be a blessing to others. God can take you to places you have never been before…He can expand your mind beyond religion. He can

also increase your territory.

THE VIRTUOUS WOMAN...

A virtuous woman is vigilant. She is an intercessor, righteous, truthful, understanding, obedient, and an overcomer. She does not compromise her values. She is sensitive to needs of others—spiritually, mentally, emotionally, financially and socially. She is wise, meek, attentive and she is nurturing.

Yolanda Marshall

THE Word of God says: "Who can find a virtuous woman for her price is far above rubies. The heart of her husband doth safely trust in her, so that he shall have no need of spoil. She will do him good and not evil all the days of her life. She seeketh wool, and flax, and worketh willingly with her hands. She is like the merchants ship; she bringeth her food from afar. She riseth also while it is yet night, and giveth meat to her household and a portion to her maidens. She considereth a field, and buyeth it; with the fruit of her hands. She planteth a vineyard. She girdeth her loins, with strength, and stregtheneth her arms.

She perceiveth that her merchandise is good. Her candle goeth not out by night. She layeth her hands to the spindle, and her hands hold the distaff. She stretcheth out her hand to the poor; yea, she reacheth forth her hands to the needy, she is not afraid of the snow for her household, for all her household are clothed with scarlet. She maketh herself coverings of tapestry; her clothing is silk and purple. Her husband is known in the gates, when he sitteth among the elders of the land. She maketh fine linen and selleth it; and delivereth girdles unto the merchant. Strength and honour are her clothing; and she shall rejoice in time to come.

She openeth her mouth with wisdom; and in her tongue is the law of kindness. She looketh well to the ways of her household, and eateth not the bread of idleness. Her children arise up, and call her blessed;

her husband also, and he praiseth her. Many daughters have done virtuously, but thou excellest them all. Favour is deceitful, and beauty is vain; but a woman that feareth the Lord, she shall be praised. Give her of the fruit of her hands; and let her own works praise her in the gates."

Proverbs 31:10-31

ACKNOWLEDGEMENT

FIRST and foremost, I give eternal thanks to my Heavenly Father for His daily presence and many provisions...for Who He is, has been, and will continue to be in my life. It is an honor to serve Him by serving others in delivering this message (His message) of hope, healing and deliverance, and new beginnings for women young and old—everywhere. Father, I thank YOU for peace, YOUR guidance, and YOUR inspiration through the many trials on my life's journey and during the course of bringing this work to fruition. Thanks for showing me the way to faith, focus, determination and victory. All honor and glory belong to YOU.

I give thanks to my mother for being a consistent example of virtue. This book would not be possible without her life as I now know it and the many experiences that she has shared with me. The understanding and mindfulness you have shown during this often challenging and demanding process will always be remembered and cherished.

To my daughter and son, Kiarra and Marvin, thank you for your patience and your understanding. Graduate school followed by this effort has meant countless hours out of your presence, yet my love and prayers were always with you. My desire to achieve these and other goals are done with you in my prayers, in my heart, and on my mind always. Thanks to you, Marvin, for leading prayers always asking God's blessings for this book to bless others...I thank God for giving me the gift of living on this side of eternity as your mother, teacher, student, mentor, and friend. Both of you helped in my profound desire to continue growing in Godly character, in essence—exemplifying the character of the woman (lady) I have been blessed to write about. I love you both so much.

Special thanks to my family for believing in me and seeing the vision. Thanks for your help! Your generosity means more than can be expressed. God bless all of you! I give a special thanks to Zack, Leah,

Tonya, and Darius. Zack, you were really encouraging during the final process of this book. Also, I give special thanks to Renay and Charles for your generosity and kind words. I give thanks to my sister, Shun, who opened her door to my children and I in our time of need. I thank you for offering your support in helping my children while I was working on this book and attending graduate school.

I give thanks to my former Pastor, Willie L. Brown Jr., of Full Gospel Fellowship Church in Pinson, Alabama. I thank God for your teachings. You shared many messages that helped me to spiritually grow. Thank you for challenging me to go to the next level so that God could use me. I want to thank you for trusting me, and giving me the opportunity to share my first message on *Virtue*. You mentioned several times that you could see the anointing on my life, beyond my mistakes. Thank you most for starting the prayer warrior team, which I was honored to have been a part of. We prayed every Saturday morning for all people. Prayer is needed, and it has truly helped me through my trials and tribulations. Prayer was also essential to writing every chapter of this book.

I also give God all the honor and glory for a dear friend, Minister Vincent Collins, who inspired me to write this book. Our friendship, although, rather young (not quite three years "young"), is a gift and truly purposed by God. It has been a wonderful journey with many lessons learned and shared. You have been a wonderful friend. You have challenged my thoughts, not only prodding me to think outside the box, but "to get outside the box and think" as you have stated so often. You have truly been there in ways that only God can get the glory. I thank God for you.

To Minister Cedric Stringer, I thank you for allowing God to use you in the spur of the moment to share a powerful message of perseverance and hope at my graduation dinner. I thank God for your preparation, even before I called you. God is truly good! Your words of encouragement meant so much to me. The "message" was one that I often reflect upon, and it has truly helped me to appreciate what Phillipians 4:13 says, "I can do all things through Christ who strengthens me." It also helped me to understand that if I can persevere, in spite of the hardship and negativity that I faced during graduate school, then I could achieve the same and taste the victory again in writing this book. I give God all the Glory!

I would like to give a special thanks to Tonya, Anita, Shundala, Phyllis and Marisa for being aspiring women of virtue and walking in it daily. Thanks for the prayers and words of encouragement through my many trials. Each of you reminded me of the call of God upon my life when it seemed there were so many things in question...God is the answer!

I cannot forget Ms. Shenita Lawson, a stranger, yet an angel from the Lord. I thank God for using you to be a blessing in my life when I needed it most—I love you for your obedience and sensitivity. Mrs. Yolanda Dickerson, you are a wonderful and giving person. I thank God for you. I give a special thanks to Mr. Erskine Daniel and his wife, author, Tracy Oneal-Daniel for all of your support. Ms. Nita, I thank you for opening your doors for the dinner that took place at your place of business in my honor. I would like to thank Mrs. Viola Broadnax for all of your help—you are a sweet, kind, and wonderful person. I must thank Mrs. Rebecca Harris who responded to the appeal of a stranger, which was to bless others. I will never forget your kindness. To Pam and Harper, thank you for being a blessing in my life. Thank you for taking my son to baseball and football practice as I wrote this book. I will always remember your generosity. I would like to thank Felix, Barry, Doc, Dorothy, Sonya, and Janice. Each of you will always hold a special place in my heart. In addition, I thank everyone else who played a part in this book being brought to fruition. I would like to give thanks to Chris Fraser at Artistic Concepts. You did a wonderful job with designing the awesome book cover. I want to also thank Bernice Guity at P & G Communications in Atlanta, Georgia for editing this book. Thanks for all of your sincere prayers and support. I pray blessings upon each of you.

FOREWORD

IF you have made the choice to read this book, then it is my belief that by the time you have read the last chapter, you will know you have taken the best step toward changing your life. You will be able to identify fundamental reasons for many of your challenges as well as the challenges of others, if you commit to meditate on the stories in the book.

Change will require total devotion to stating the affirmations and referring to those specific to whatever negative thoughts and feelings or circumstances you are faced with (stemming from your past or otherwise). You must commit them to memory and repeat them aloud once per day in order to transform your thoughts.

It is my sincere hope that you will find the prayers throughout this book comforting. I hope they serve as the premise for opening a line of communication with the Heavenly Father, geared toward sharing your deepest hurts, pains, disappointments, even your fears. The prayers will also help you uncover any hidden unforgiveness, envy, strife, or judgment toward others. In order to move forward, these issues must be addressed and removed. I share with the author, the belief that deliverance and healing start with locating suppressed feelings, while abandoning the tendency to deny those issues you are totally aware of being sold out to admitting and sharing, openly, the truth of these issues through honest confession.

A personal definition of confession is offered in honor of new beginnings. That definition is courageously and clearly speaking outwardly, the truth about things mistaken. It also involves knowingly or unknowingly holding that truth painfully or wrongfully inside.

Here, you will learn the concept of three-fold Confessions, a term she inspired stemming from countless conversations with her about the steps taken in the process of her advancing from being a victim to a victor —recognized, in essence, as being central to Christian counseling, secular and/or clinical approaches to mental and emotional healing.

By being totally open and honest with yourself and communicating these issues to God, will help you advance toward the two relationships (REALATIONSHIPS) that are key to initial, and then permanent change...two relationships always in reach but seemingly so far out of reach in whole or in part perhaps for many years: your relationship to God, your relationship with yourself—founded upon His love, grace, mercy, favor, forgiveness, peace.

This book is the product of an undying passion to share a message of hope and endless possibilities of wholeness with women of every walk of life who have walked through life as broken, shattered, and battered vessels. The author, unselfish in her quest, reaches out to others with outstretched arms that reflect her thanks to God for reaching out to her; for those persons He ordained to reach out to her on her journey. And to this new place you, too, will soon discover and take refuge in.

The author will guide you toward releasing the "negatives" to make room for the real you—filled with the goodness of the Father's Spirit and all the blessings. Yolanda continues to be unwavering in her desire to live and direct by being an example of the seeds for change offered through this special work—not just a presenter of worthy ideals.

Minister Vincent Collins

PREFACE

IN late September 2006, I am not sure of the exact date but I remember it being a sunny day, my friend and I were sitting at Civitan Park, in Center Point, Alabama. Our conversation was briefly interrupted by a thought. This was a very different kind of thought. Although I had had this thought before, this time it was different. This thought seemed to be bigger, clearer, infused by a profound passion, coupled with a sense of direction.

After praying over the years and seeking God only a few days before and a few moments prior to this moment—that still small voice had spoken. I had heard it. I had received it. It was clear. I had moved from *believing* to *knowing* the work that I have been purposed to do could be found in my triumphs over many trials. At that moment, I knew without a doubt that God had been conditioning me to be a blessing to women from all walks of life that represent every kind of brokenness. All I had gone through—from conception to this point—was moving me in a direction of surrender to God and commitment to serve others.

I started to write my first book in 2001, which was not completed. However, this assignment was one that had to be brought to fruition. For this book is a gift from God through me to you. My hope and prayer is that you will find it an answer to your prayers, reason to believe in life, love, happiness, and wholeness that you will gladly share with others. Life needs you…welcomes…embraces you…is you…would not be the same without you. For you, this book was written. To you this book is presented from a friend who knows well that things are possible to you as you grow to believe that all things are possible with God who is not only worthy of your belief, but your knowing.

From *Victim to Virtuous* is your book. It is our book. And a *Virtuous Woman* is who you are beyond all you have been through. Although you may have been or still are identified with many of the mistakes you have made, poor decisions, or even for your lifestyle—this is not your true identity. Who are you? Above all, you are God's child.

INTRODUCTION

ONE of the most blessed gifts of all is the desire of a woman to claim LADY status. This separates you from any other name that is given...that is to say *A VIRTUOUS WOMAN*. A "LADY" is often the title or identification placed upon and is associated with: those with a desire for, unwavering commitment to values and morals measured by godly standards that never change. The external, sacred, spiritual truths of the Bible are such standards. In one word—*virtue*. I have come to appreciate virtue as a virtuous woman, a "LADY." In Proverbs 22:1 we read, "A good name is rather to be chosen than great riches, and loving favour rather than silver and gold."

For all women were born with the seed of virtue. When the seed is nourished and watered daily, it allows us to grow into the tree that produces good fruit. A woman of virtue positively affects everyone in her world from her household to her community, from her place of employment to even strangers she might come in contact with in passing.

There will be storms in life that seem to threaten the very existence as a tree of virtue. Nonetheless, you have been chosen by the Father to stand and bear healthy fruit. With every storm comes a new challenge. The fierce winds have caused many of us to bend a little or even a lot, but we did not break; we are still here! The storms may have come in the form of mental, emotional, social, physical, even spiritual abuse. Many are the violations of that which lead to brokenness—for one molestation...for another the disloyalty of someone you trusted with your life...for another constant verbal abuse—nothing can destroy us unless we submit to the destroyer. And many have made it through and are whole and/or on the road to recovery toward wholeness.

Often you do not realize how strong you are. Some of most anointed, powerful, creative, successful women today were once victims in yesterday, but they are whole now. Many who now take the center stage in ministry and other fields of endeavor were once hidden in the shadow of guilt, shame...brokenness. Through faith, perseverance, and discovering a definite purpose in life—scores of ladies through the ages have reclaimed their lives and proven that being an overcomer, more than a conqueror, has more to do with one's mindset than setbacks.

There are several well-known women of God who were once broken, but each of them had the desire to love themselves, and most of all they love God. As they have broken free to bless others, so will you. Oprah Winfrey, one of my favorites, and one of the most beloved television personalities of all times, moved from being a victim to virtuous. I have been deeply blessed and inspired by her story. She has blessed millions, not only through the resourcefulness of her show covering a broad range of topics—she also gives generously to the less fortunate, under privileged, through many efforts to share the simple truth that make life more livable and enjoyable.

There are many other stories of women throughout the ages that will forever be examples of the personal freedom and many successes that result from spiritual, mental, emotional, social, and spiritual growth. Love, faith, wisdom, understanding, knowledge, obedience—Action! You must move toward a better you. *Please remember that faith and prayer is the foundation for change, but action is required for change.*

The Bible also makes mention of several women of virtue—Sara, Ruth, Esther, Mary, Hannah, just to name a few—and these women had faith, too! Oh, and I cannot forget my favorite, the woman at the well. This was the woman who they brought to Jesus to be stoned. Based on their thoughts and description of this woman, she was not a virtuous woman, not a lady, yet this woman was birthed into life with the seed of virtue. She was no less of a woman than those mentioned. In fact, Jesus saw the intentions of her heart. He told her to go and sin no more. But one thing for sure, those hypocrites were not found without sin...so what did that make them?

A story in the Bible concerns a woman who had an issue of blood (an issue with impurities in the blood that caused multiple problems).

She had this issue for twelve years. She thought that if she touched the hem of Jesus' garment she would be made whole. She made up her mind to do so, and did. Faith coupled with action brought her healing and deliverance—wholeness. Hannah had faith that God would open up her womb so that she could bear a male child. Sara had faith in knowing that she could have a child in her old age. Ruth had faith in knowing that God was preparing a king—Boaz—for her sensitivity to Naomi, obedience, and virtue. Ruth had longed for the companionship of a righteous man for many years. Boaz was not just a man; he was "the man"—the king for this queen of hearts.

These are just a few faith stories mentioned in the Bible, and examples of people with faith and action with respect to surrendering their wants and desires over to God and allowing His will to be done in their lives. Faith, opposite of fear, is what pleases God and moves you in a direction toward what you believe. Faith is about believing to see—not seeing is believing. It is about thinking and developing a clear picture in your mind of who you desire to be—what you desire to have—who it is to honor and glorify God and bless others—actions that allow you to some day drop the shackles of brokenness or confusion and be free to live as He intended. I knew bondage—yet I now know freedom and wholeness. It was faith that brought me; experiences that taught me; wisdom that guided me; the Spirit of God who protects me; meekness that grounds me.

I have always believed that a person could be delivered. I didn't know when, but I did know why. Why? Because freedom and virtue is God's will. I now thank Him for what I have been through. He has given me gifts that money cannot buy. He has given me Himself—His Love—His Word—wisdom—spiritual gifts—and a deep desire for virtue.

"Now faith is the substance of things hoped for, the evidence of things not seen."
(Hebrews 11:1)

Now before you go on I would like to offer this prayer: *Lord, help us to love, surrender, and see each other and ourselves through your eyes—based on love not judgment. Allow us to see each other as being made in your image. Father, help us all to fear less and love more. Allow us to pray for each other's shortcomings rather than judge. Help us to see that many of the destructive patterns and behavior are the manifestation of a mind and soul infested with brokenness. Let us not look down on one another for lack of material or education, looks or any other issue that is contrary to who you say we are. Whether dark skin or light skin, whether brown skin or white skin. Whether tall or short, thin or overweight—we are not our looks; we are spiritual beings engaged in becoming the masters in our experiences as human beings. We are spirits and women becoming more like you—virtuous. Unforgiveness, jealously, hate, envy, fear, poor self-image, and other doubts must be eliminated. We will not glorify any woman, man, or child—only You deserve all the glory. Amen.*

I have written this book to share with all women, saved or unsaved. All of us can possess the characteristics of a virtuous woman and become our best to God's glory. He sees where you are now, and knows your end. God reigns on the just as well as the unjust, and we must always remember that.

My prayer is that this book will help shed light on the dark areas of women's lives, helping them to find themselves in light of who they can be and have been purposed to be. The path to truth and deliverance to gain freedom is for everyone. If you are virtuous, but broken, I am sure this book will help guide you in a direction of becoming that whole, virtuous woman. So many of us can identify with the challenges that life has presented to us, but if we would be open and share with each other, we can help build stronger girls and boys, other women and men, and defeat the enemy on every hand.

PART ONE

MY journey in essence does not start with me. My journey starts with my mother who realized that she was the product of a journey before she was my mother. I always knew there was something special about my mother. Well, actually, there are 12 others who also call her mother. She was definitely being fruitful. My mother would be the first to rise in the morning and the last to lie down at night. She was prayerful, generous and sensitive. She truly had the gift of virtue. She was a virtuous woman, BUT...

I can never do justice to my mother's virtue—well, the dynamics of my mother's virtue—without mentioning my dad. Her husband! Yes, he was! He died in 1997, but my memory of him is long lasting. He was tall and handsome, with those gray eyes. A good man he was, yet he was also abusive, fussy, angry...and most of all he was controlling. He was full of energy and laughter. I loved my dad! He loved his children, too. But he had a strange way of showing his love. He was a provider, yet we were living in poverty. We will take a deeper look at this later.

I now realize my mother was a symbol of virtue, but nonetheless broken. She was very strong, yet paradoxically weakened by brokenness. This was the foundation by which life began to build the person that I am today. To understand who I am today, we have to open the Pandora's Box of the journey called: *My Life.*

When I was a little girl, I would get on my knees every night and pray, *"Thou lay me down to sleep I pray to the Lord my soul to keep, if I should die before I wake, I pray to the Lord my soul to take."* As a child, I took that prayer very seriously because I really did not think I was going to wake up after having those bad dreams of my mother being beaten by my father, and those giant rats crawling in our bedroom. I could barely go to sleep—all I heard was his loud voice calling my mother everything, but a child of God—you...you...you. I could not tell which one was worse—his loud voice or the rats squeaking throughout the night. My father even called us, the children, bad names, too.

Every morning I was awakened by the smell of my mother's good ole southern breakfast. Biscuits, eggs, and bacon were my favorite breakfast food items. When I opened my eyes, the first things I saw were feet...right by my mouth—the feet of one of my sisters. There were three of us to one bed. The bedroom was small. Two beds could barely fit in the room. We had one dresser for our clothing, which obviously was not enough space for the tees, panties and socks of six little girls (and two more to come later). Everything that could not fit in the drawers was stored in garbage bags and placed in the closet.

We had to rise very early each morning because there was only one bathroom for the girls and boys. We had to make it quick when it was our turn because there were so many of us. While exiting the bathroom, I could hear the voice of my sister, "Landa, what are you going to wear today?" I answered, "I don't know." Then, I would go through the bags and pull out something that had already been worn by one of my sisters the day before.

After everyone got dressed, prayed over our food, and ate, we would yell, "See you later, Mom and Dad! We'll see y'all this evening!" Out the door we went. As we were on our way to school, I could not help but think about what my mom had told us about our behavior and making good grades. She was serious about each of her children earning an education. She did not play about slacking in our school work. We all knew you better not bring a bad grade home or that was your butt!

My mother made sure we did our homework when we arrived home each evening. Oftentimes she would pop up at the school. You had to be on your best behavior all the time because you did not know when she would show up unannounced. Coupled with the high expectations of our making "high marks" on our schoolwork was equally as high an expectation to be on our best behavior. Good grades and bad behavior were not tolerated. Even with all of her encouragement, some of us still slacked in making good grades, and being on our best behavior. But I could not just think about my mom's expectations of our making good grades. In addition, I thought about the humiliation that I was about to face from classmates that recognized I was wearing the same outfit my sister wore the day before. You know, it was typical for the sisters to wear each other's clothes. Oh, do not mention other things they decided to find wrong with me...my hair, my shoes, my looks...so it was rather hard to focus on making good grades when I really did not want to be there. I knew that I was going to face this issue every day until something changed.

And looking through a child's eye, I did not see our situation getting any better. Poverty seemed to have overtaken us, and not only poverty. Unfortunately, I did not see my mother or father getting dressed for work each morning. "How are things going to get better?" I asked. Well, now I can see why my mom could not work a 9-to-5 job. Her full-time job was to raise her children. My father's monthly veteran's check was the only income, and it barely provided our needs.

Now wearing each other's clothes was not the only typical thing. It was also typical for me to wear a face of hurt and awe. This stemmed from the restless, unpeaceful, and unforgettable nights. Oftentimes strange things would happen between sunset and sunrise. You know those types of things that so many of us have gone through, not able to tell anyone—maybe even you. To tell someone the truth about this situation, often means that the innocent are told something in response, which can make you feel like everything and anything, but a child of God. And you are often called a liar and made to feel that if something did happen—which they do not believe happened—it is all your fault. The innocent are often made to suffer for peace sake.

The older I became, the worse I felt. I knew that I was going to face so many familiar faces that did not quite understand the true essence of my position—how I was living—how I was violated—and how this affected me.

As stated before, my father only received a government check that seemingly was not enough to get us out of poverty. I remember my father doing handy work every now and again, a couple of times a month—maybe three or more. I heard he had his own heating business, but that was before my time. I am not certain what happened to my father's business. But my father had the strangest kind of hustle, and he involved his children. He said that he knew of a way to earn extra money. After he shared it with us, I thought his idea was really scary.

I had just started high school, and I wanted to enjoy my teenage years. Seemingly, the weekends were the only time I could think about having fun because mom wanted us to focus on our school work during the week. While I was thinking about having the teenage fun on the weekends, not necessarily run the streets but have that freedom to enjoy my sisters, brothers, and our close friends—my father had another plan in mind.

This was the earning "extra money" plan. He would order huge amounts of donuts for us to sell in the strangest, yet dangerous places—the liquor stores. As I looked at this picture through a child's eye, I knew something was not right. My siblings also knew something was wrong with this! If we ever asked him the question, "Why do we have to go to the liquor stores to sell donuts?" He would cuss us out completely. With that in mind, we had no option. Well, I guess we did have options. And that was choosing which liquor store we wanted to stand in front of to sell donuts. We were taught to be obedient. But this time it was very hard to submit to his rules.

We would gather around the room and talk about who would pair up for which liquor store. "Which one do you want to go to?" I asked my sister. Hurry up! The decision needs to be made quickly because you know Mom and Dad will be back in a few minutes, and he is going to be ready to load up.

Sure enough, when Dad arrived with the trunk filled with donuts, you better have been ready to load up or that was your butt. He would get out of the car and come in the house, "Are y'all ready?" He asked. Well, if we were not ready, he would just put us into pairs. One of my sisters and I were standing in the front room when he said, "I'm taking y'all to Avondale liquor store." He told the other siblings, "Your mom and I will be back to pick y'all up. There's not enough room in the car."

It only took us about 10 minutes to get to our destination. The frowns on our faces did not last long. Once we arrived, we drove to the side of the building, started unloading the donuts, and positioned ourselves on the small brick attached to the building that could barely hold us up. "Smile," "Smile," he would say as he drove off. "I'll be back to pick y'all up in a couple of hours. But if y'all finish before I get back, just call me." I felt as though my own father was using us. If you are thinking what my mom had to say about all of this, well, sometimes she also had to go with us.

I can remember the disappointing look on my sister's face. We were both unhappy. It was very embarrassing because we always saw someone we knew each time we had to go. Ironically, some of our classmates would show up with their relatives. We felt as though we were so alone. We thought to ourselves: "What can we do?" We can't run…we can't dodge…and we can't even hide.

The shame we felt when we had to dodge the children we went to school with, and those in the neighborhoods, were fresh on our minds. It was as fresh as the donuts. The only difference is the shame lasted longer than the boxes of donuts we were selling. Each Monday, I could only pray that I would not be criticized at school.

After this so-called hustle was being repeated every weekend, the question was asked to my mother this time. "Why do we have to go to the liquor stores to sell donuts?" She replied, "I have to go, too! That's your dad who's got y'all out there." We had to ask her everything in secret because my dad was so controlling.

The sad part of this hustle was lying about the church. Yes, my dad told us to lie about the church! We had to tell the customers we were selling donuts for our church. Actually, I was not a member of a church at the time, but some of my siblings were. The question was asked, "Why lie about the church?" He said, "They would not know. Most of those customers may not ask anyway. Their minds are on drinking that whiskey." Well, sure enough, one Sunday morning my sister's pastor announced that someone had been standing in front of liquor stores lying about the church. Oh, what an embarrassment it was—somebody must have told!

Yeah, speaking of my dad's response to the customer's having their minds on drinking that whiskey…One day, my sister and I were standing in front of the liquor store, and we approached an angry male customer and asked, "Hi, Mr. Would you like to buy a box of donuts or give a donation to our church?" He said, "No. I don't want to buy any (blank) donuts." Well, he was full of whiskey and he was going to buy more. I wish you could have seen the look on his face when my sister asked him if he wanted to buy some donuts. He just started attacking her. I was so scared. I did not know what to do. I was only 14 years old. My sister started crying and I panicked.

She told me to run across the street to the store to call my dad. I wanted so badly for her to go with me, but she did not want to leave the donuts in front of the store. I called my dad to tell him what happened. He was so angry with us. He said, "I just dropped y'all (blank) off." I said, "But this man is attacking her." Sadly, he did not arrive until much later when it was close for the store to close.

The seeds of frustration, agitation, confusion, anger and resentment were planted within me. Some of my siblings also felt this way. After seeing the physical and mental abuse of my mother and siblings, it was hard for me to receive my father. Although I still loved him, I was so ready to move from under his roof. When I started my junior year in high school, I started counting down the days that remained under this roof. This was also the year I turned 16 years old, so I was permitted to date.

I realize that when a woman's life is controlled by anyone other than God and she does not clearly know who she is, chances are she will go through life with a distorted view of love and a false sense of who she is, and it has a way of tainting any hopes of being free to become all she can be. My mother is beautiful, and she is a woman of virtue, as so many women are today. My mother has often found herself succumbing to the fierce waters of influence from a controlling man.

When anyone yields to the influence of another, whether it is negative or positive, and they are your leader, it has a way of trickling down to the innocent minds of those who are watching—the followers. In this case, I am talking about the children. When a child sees her mother or father being influenced by the control of anyone, they will grow accustomed to this behavior that can spill over into their relationships when they become adults. They will find themselves being influenced by their peers as children. This can play a major role in them letting others think for them. When this happens, they are being taught to be followers, not leaders.

What I went through as a child definitely had an impact on my adulthood, as much as my childhood. I had developed the following mentality. I was confused and broken. My brokenness led to many dysfunctional relationships until I was made whole. When I was a child I had observed my parent's behavior, which I thought was good behavior. Much of what I thought was good behavior is what had me blind and confused for so long.

Just imagine how something can look good on the outside, but it is really bad on the inside. In this case, I am talking about people and how they behave. When we execute bad or good behavior, it often stems from what is on the inside of us. Mind you, what is on the inside of you will come out sooner or later. Ask yourself, "Why do I act a certain way? Is it as a result of what is on the inside of me?" I found myself questioning my parent's behavior. *Why was there so much chaos and confusion in the home? Why was my father so angry and bitter? Why did he use so many disparaging words toward his family? Why did my mother accept so much abuse?* I had my reasons for questioning their behavior because I was affected by it. After long prayers and constant meditation, I was afforded the truth. The truth of where my brokenness stemmed from. I hope you are not confused. Let me give you an example of where I am trying to take you.

Say you have an apple and an orange, and they both look good on the outside, but they are rotten on the inside. You do not really find out they are rotten until you take a bite. Here is the thing, before you take a bite; you kind of have that feeling that something is wrong with both pieces of fruit because you have had them for quite some time in your fruit tray inside of your refrigerator. Since you have taken a bite out of them, you find out what you were really feeling about these two pieces of fruit was true.

I had observed the marriage of two people (my mother and father) who seemed happy on the outside, but broken on the inside. In seeking truth, it was as though I had taken a bite out of an apple, and it was rotten (broken), and then an orange that was the same. When you have two pieces of fruit that you are expecting to experience a sweet, good taste from—with the greatest benefit being Vitamin C (wholeness), yet all you get is "rot," it was through this reality, coupled with observing my siblings, that God was able to gently speak to the brokenness that was within me, hold my hand, and lead me on a path of understanding, forgiveness, hope and wisdom. He also gave me the power to overcome what could have remained a setback, a permanent negative dilemma. He used it to move me from being a victim to a victor of virtue.

I thank Him for leading me to truth about where my brokenness stemmed from, by allowing me to reflect on my childhood to connect the dots and make sense out of the life that He has so preciously given me—a life full of laughter, joy, peace, purpose and destiny. To be a leader and not a follower! I am so thankful for all of His goodness. I am going to share with you some of the major events that turned my life around—toward my purpose—all by the grace of God.

PART TWO

WE should talk now about those dysfunctional relationships that I had submitted to and which led to decisions that resulted in me bringing two children into this world —all due to my brokenness. We should also talk about how these relationships distracted me from focusing on what God had intended for me and how they played a big part in my going down paths that seemingly hindered my spiritual, emotional, social, financial, and mental growth. One of the most important things to remember and give attention to in this matter, as stated before, is that I was 16 years old when I was permitted to date.

From my first relationship, the first guy I dated (the one who I had my firstborn child with) up to the second marriage and divorce at the age of 31, I had been in transition. I went from man to man. I went into these relationships looking through the eyes of my parents. That is to say, the only things they seemed to have been able to see and value was money and material provisions. Never mind the emotional, spiritual, mental sensitivity, and provision was all about what I have come to call the "M and M" provision, *"Money and Material."*

I found myself accepting any type of behavior simply because I was looking for just one thing in a man (M and M), and I thought it was the right thing to do. But once I submitted to such behavior, everything that was hidden on the inside of him eventually showed its face during the relationship. It is what hindered me and kept me going backwards year after year, one relationship at a time. This happened because I allowed myself to become emotionally attached each time I entered a new relationship. I was a person who struggled with low self-esteem for many years, so it was not easy to walk away each time, no matter how bad the relationship was.

I was 17 years young, confused, and broken when I had my first child. I did not know anything about mothering a child because I was still a child myself. I was a senior in high school, trying to take care of a baby that I did not have full knowledge of how to nurture, other than change the diaper and feed her a bottle when she would cry. I also cannot forget that I did have to get up with her throughout the night. My mother and father enforced this because they said I had made my bed hard, so I had to lay in it. They would so often say this.

I was not financially able to take care of a child. The welfare system was all I knew, just like so many of the young girls and ladies I saw as I was growing up. I applied for welfare and food stamps so that I could provide for my daughter. I was amazed that I could only receive $137 per month in welfare. Clearly, this was not enough to take care of a child. Besides, I was nearly grown, and my parents could barely support me; and they certainly could not afford to feed another mouth and all of the other necessary obligations.

My child was my full responsibility. I had made an adult's decision with a child's mind. Because of this decision, my parents were forced to play the mother and father role in my absence, while I attended high school. Although I had not graduated from high school, I had the responsibilities of a mother when I came home each day from school. There was no mistake about this! I had to act the role that I created for myself as a mother. The consequences of my decision immediately came into play. I will never forget those restless nights as a high school student having to take on this kind of adult responsibility. *Can you imagine how that could have felt?* I had to stay up every night to feed my baby, rock her to sleep, and then rise very early to go to school the next morning. This is my story! This might even be your story, but it does not have to be. This is the consequence of choice.

I can even remember having to catch that big, yellow school bus every morning, right across from Whatley Elementary School. There were six or more of us waiting for the bus to arrive around 7:15 a.m. I stayed to myself as we stood there waiting for the bus to arrive. Each of us who waited for the bus was from different backgrounds, but we had so much in common. We were all very young, and each of us carried a child that we could not possibly take care of at such a young age. I was not perfect and I had not mastered my mothering skills, but it was apparent that the majority of the other young mothers also had no clue. Some girls are purposed to be mothers. Others can learn to be mothers. *But it is clear by the vast number of children who are misguided and troubled, the lack of parenting, wisdom, loving, and nurturing is at the root.*

As we would load the bus, often I would think about and ask myself, *"Why are so many young girls even having babies?"* I now understand and I have some of the answers. Could it be a cycle? Did the mother have her first baby at a young age? Could it be because of peer pressure? Could it be because of what is shown on the television? Could it be because of what is heard on the radio? I will have to say "Yes!" to each of these questions. Just take a look around you.

I had many thoughts of dropping out of school because I did not have any parenting skills I needed. Although I have always had a mothering spirit (that does make a difference), yet I was new to the mothering experience. I still had to learn how to become a mother. It is fair to say that my parents and others always recognized me as a nurturer, even when I was very young. My dad would always say, "There's something special about Landa. She has a good heart."

I always wanted to help people. I was always in the kitchen helping my mother prepare meals for the entire family. I also helped take care of my younger siblings. As I look back, dedication, patience, wisdom, and unconditional mother's love is definitely what was, and still is, required to raise children. The wisdom of God has taught me how to become the mother I have been purposed to be, in spite of the fact that I had my first child at a young age.

My pregnancy was embarrassing. I knew so many girls my age, those who I walked to school with, who were focused on their education and going to college. Because of my pregnancy, I did not have a clear view of going to college. I did not realize how it could have impacted my life positively. But I am thankful for my sister, Cathy, who encouraged me to finish high school because there were only a few months remaining before graduation. Believe me! I really needed encouragement during this time in my life.

My first child was born three months before my high school graduation. I graduated in 1991. All of my hope of going to college had totally faded. I did not want to leave my baby to go to college. Although I still maintained the value of education, which my mother had instilled in me and my siblings, the decision to delay attending college was one of my circumstances. My hope and focus was to be there for my baby until she was older.

Do you remember me telling you about how I was ready to get out from under my father's roof? Well, the time had come. I was just turning 18 years old, when my child's father and I moved in together. We moved into this community which appeared to be safe, but later realized that we were surrounded by several people who had drug habits; these people seemingly did not go to sleep. Now moving in with a man was definitely something new for me. If there was one thing I remember always being told besides you need a provider, it was that you do not need to shack up with a man. Now those two things I had heard clearly. I had heard this advice ever since I could remember. Yet, this new place in my life offered something my parents, and most adults, repeatedly expressed: Provision. This, I will always remember. The decision for me to live with my child's father was a high-impact decision that has had an impact on my life in ways that only in recent years I have been blessed to truly understand.

This was a tough decision for me, but at that time I was just ready to move. And I thought my child's father could potentially offer me M and M (*money and material*) as he proved to do as a young qualified provider. Yet, there was more. I did not quite know all that love was supposed to be. The kind of love that my father had shown all my life was both hurtful at times, and confusing. What I did know is that I, as well as my daughter, needed the love of a man who was not angry, verbally abusive, or would mentally drain me. However, what I failed to realize is that the hurting child on the inside of me had not yet been healed.

I experienced real love all right. As time progressed, it seems as though I was reliving my childhood experience of love as I had done under my father's roof. Now this was a different roof, but things seemed so familiar. Just as I had seen my father hustle to make a living and "provide" by having us sell donuts in front of liquor stores, placing us in harm's way, this was a new representation of a conflicting past which had placed all of my siblings in danger. Yes, it was quite dangerous. Well, with my child's father, I was forced to be involved in a different kind of hustle {drug dealing}—a different kind of danger.

The danger of this hustle came into play soon after it started. One night I found myself fighting to go to sleep as my child's father left to work the graveyard shift, leaving my daughter and me alone with his cousin to carry out his hustle. As I tossed and turned, I found myself lying on my left side, and I could see his cousin entering my dark bedroom, as the reflection of the moonlight shined through my window, making it obvious for me to capture the view of a gun being held to his back by another man. Yes, he was being robbed—everything he had, to what was stored in our bedroom had been taken. Now here I am pretending to be asleep, yet shaking and praying that God will deliver me from this unsafe environment.

This incident was followed by another time when a stranger hid behind our kitchen wall waiting with his gun for the first person breathing to come home—he was in motion to rob us. The very next day, my child's father was upset I did not come home the night this occurred (I felt a deep yearning within to stay away on this night). He expressed that this man indeed tried to rob him and there was a great struggle between the two of them, both firing their guns as the stranger fled the scene.

This was the kind of hustle that required me to dodge when necessary, find a hiding place, and sleep with one eye open. Speaking of sleeping with one eye open, it was true that I could only sleep with one eye open for at least a week because I could not open my left eye. My child's father had kicked me in my left eye with his steel-toed boots that he was wearing on the night of this fighting match. This happened shortly after we split up. I guess that was better than having my brains blown out with a nine-millimeter Glock that he held between my eyes threatening to kill me, then himself. He was doing this because I had found interest in somebody else who I thought could love me better, trying to escape all this madness of the sleepless nights, uninvited strangers—the robbers, addictive customers…it was not the best way to escape, nonetheless, it was time.

Let me say this—facing a gun was not anything new for me. The first person who pulled a gun on me was my father. He pulled a rifle on me. One day, I went over to visit my parents, only to find them in a heated argument—this was not new either. The argument stemmed from my father's decision to give one of my brothers' girlfriend money to get her hair fixed, instead of one of my sisters. I know you are probably thinking, *her brother's girlfriend*? Yes, he divided the brothers and sisters when we were children; even now the spirit of division exists within our family. My father would imply, *my sons will always carry my name, and my daughters will carry somebody else's name*. In essence, he was saying that he would take care of my brothers' girlfriends/wives before he would take care of his own daughters. This was really silly; nonetheless, it was stated numerous times. Now on the day this madness occurred, at least half of us were all grown up and dating. But on this particular day, the verbal abuse, which consisted of bad name calling (a female dog), was not done just in front of family anymore. It was done in the presence of one of my brothers' girlfriend.

But my mother had now gained some energy (she spoke a peace of her mind) to defend her children after many years of our family being abused, namely her daughters. Not only did my mother gain energy to defend her children, I found myself defending my mother this day by standing up for what was right. Well, as I stood up for what was right, I was wronged by having to dodge a bullet as I drove my red Nissan Sentra off the curb in fear of being shot by my father, coupled with risking being hit by a car head on because I was watching the gun instead of the street. Now I was facing two endangerments at the same time. I was not the only one in danger; one of my younger sisters was in the car with me.

What another sad image to identify with love! "Was this love?" This is the question I had been asking seemingly all my life. I was ready to experience this thing called real, love. I found out it was not in material things because my child's father gave me all of that. It was not in the money. I had a substantial amount of that, too. I had been cussed out, fussed at, had a gun pulled on me, and called bad names by my father, so I knew it could not have been in that. But the question was asked, "How can someone love you—unconditionally, if they don't love themselves?"

I had dated this "provider" for more than five years. He was definitely my high school sweetheart. After he had created an environment obviously not safe for my child and me, with all the chaos, confusion, and abuse—I knew it was time for me to move on.

So, I met a friend who I thought could love me better. Yes, this was the man I had met toward the end of my first relationship. I did not even think about recovery. We started a relationship that lasted for about a year. There I was, in transition. As we were approaching a year of dating, he formed another relationship outside of ours. *"Was that love?"* I asked myself. No, it was not love! So, that relationship ended. So many questions went through my mind. What does the world have to offer me? Can it offer me love? Can I find a man in the world who can love me? How naïve I was.

When I reached adulthood, at the age of 21, which is the age I have always considered to be that of an adult, I was introduced to what the world had to offer. Yes, I was interested! I began partying—you could not keep me out of the club. I started doing things out of my character, which was totally contrary to the way I had been raised—drinking, smoking, and simulating things I saw other people doing. "Was this me?" I asked. No, no, no! I was still young, confused and broken, and I had a baby. I could not possibly find love in the world.

What I did find was a man whose eyes fell upon me as I walked to my car around 3:00 a.m. as I was leaving the club dressed like I was trying to catch a man. I was wearing shorts that nearly showed my bottom, a halter-top that revealed more of my flesh, and I cannot forget those three-inch heels. After this man had approached me—with those brown eyes and standing about 6 foot 3 tall —he shared that he had noticed me in the club. I was thinking to myself: *"This might be the kind of man I need. He is handsome. He is older. He seems to be mature. You know, he might know how to treat a lady.* The question was, "Was I being a lady?"

Shortly after that night, we started to communicate. I felt the need to share with him the experiences I had in my prior relationships. He seemed to have been very concerned. He listened, although there was more. Strangely, I had attracted a compulsive lying, manipulative, controlling man who only loved my body. I was silly to think he wanted anything more. Nonetheless, I found myself in another relationship. About a year later, this relationship ended. I realized he had something in common with the other men I had dated. All of them had a lack of respect for women. After this relationship came to a close, I asked myself, *"When am I going to meet the right man?"*

I will take you a little further—another relationship—another transition—and another child brought into this brokenness that was still within me. At the age of 23, I gave birth to my second child. This was a different father, but similar characteristics. This was very challenging for me because I did not want to fit in this group of having baby after baby with different fathers. I grew up in a house with 12 siblings, with the same father, so this was very hard for me. Besides, I wanted to be married with my second child, but this could not happen because I did not want to marry anyone who had the characteristics of my father.

I was young with two babies. Nonetheless, I was in transition again. I had even met the father of my second child in the club. He seemed very nice, but he represented that part of my father that was very good at describing women as female dogs. So this relationship ended after three years of often being labeled as a "female dog." I know you are probably asking yourself, "What was she thinking?" Well, the truth is, I was not thinking. I was searching in all the wrong places, looking for what only God could give. It was also nothing new to be called a "female dog." I had heard this since I was a child—so that was the "norm."

I was thankful for my second child but I realized I chose the route of partying instead of continuing my education. Continuing my education would have closed not only the learning gaps that existed between the ages of 17 and 23 (as I later realized in pursuing my bachelor's degree), but would have potentially helped me to focus my attention more positively. I am not saying that going to college would have prevented me from having another child, but I do believe that my focus would have been more in harmony with overall progress. By this I mean the principles instilled in me as a child concerning education would have been more likely thought upon if that choice had been made. But like most young folk, I wanted to at least try this thing they called, "partying."

After partying for years, long enough to have received my bachelor's degree, I was going nowhere and made a high-impact decision to simply shift my focus—change my life. I was partying and seeking love from those who did not know love themselves, so they could not possibly offer it. I wanted to escape the hurt by having fun, which consisted of drinking and an occasional smoke of "natural herb," all of which had taken a toll on me. Not long after this, I found myself drunk on hopes and dreams of making a better life for my family and high off all the possibilities of achieving my goals.

At this point, my heart, mind, and soul where united in truth. The truth was, I was not living life as the person and mother I was purposed to be. So, I decided to go to college, and I started in August 1998. I went full-time for years until I received my bachelor's degree in 2002. As a single mother, I knew I wanted to offer my children more than a lifestyle of partying every weekend. But one thing I struggled with was being with a man. I felt as though I needed a man. These transitions continued.

At the age of 26, I got married for the first time. I thought he was the love of my life. He was financially stable, a provider and good looking. Sounds a bit like my father, huh? You could not tell me anything. I was affectionate, intimate, and I cooked, cleaned, washed his clothes, ironed his work uniforms, delivered his lunch, took care of the children, prayed over the family, and much more. In essence, I was being my mother. That is, loving, caring, giving, and recognizing the importance of submitting to my mate. In reality, I was denied the experience of true love. I gave so much love, but it was not reciprocated.

Let me tell you though, I nagged, fussed, and complained. Now that was not healthy at all. I was an angry woman. I had to have the last word. In Proverbs 21:19 we read, "It's better to dwell in the wilderness, than with a contentious and angry woman." Well, that is just what he started doing—coming home late, cheating, and not spending quality time with the family.

I realized that I shared some of the characteristics of my father, too. The fussing and anger that I was used to seeing had spilled over into my relationships and marriage. I was still bruised on the inside from my childhood. The marriage had started to fade. My husband and I both contributed to the diminishing of our marriage. We both had our share of issues we had to battle and deal with. The complaining, nagging and fussing just did not go with the lack of spending quality time and cheating. Circumstances forced us to separate in September 2001.

Six months later, I found myself opening up to another relationship—broken and confused. There I was, in transition again. Not only that, I was not even divorced yet from the existing marriage. What was important to me at that time was just having a friendship. I wanted someone to spend quality time with, but I saw someone who was very appealing to my natural eyes. He was tall and handsome. Financially stable? Well, after the experience with my husband, it just did not matter. That is what brokenness and accepting without setting godly standards will do for you.

Was he a provider? Yes, he was a provider, but not as my father and other men in my relationships had been. He, this prince charming, provided something uniquely different. He could have a decent conversation covering a broad range of subjects, laugh and joke. God seemed to be one of our favorite topics. Did I consult God about this friendship? Not right off. Did I think about my children? No. Well, that should have been the most important concern, but I was absolutely selfish. I admit that.

Can a man be in your life and not in your children's life? Yes, this is possible. Was the inner man or spirituality important to me? Yes, and since then I have come to know that conversation is one thing, faith—practicing what we preach—is another. A person knows a tree by the fruit it bears, right? Could I have lived by myself? Yes. Would I advise women to ultimately wait on God? Yes. I have now learned that it is important to fall in love with Him in your singleness. Read on!

After a year and a half of dating this man, I was saying, "I do" for the second time. I reluctantly said "I do!" I did it anyway although I was clearly warned and convinced that this was not the man for me. Okay, ladies, I was disobedient, but I will discuss that later. You know sometimes you just have to learn the hard way, as my mother would say. I heard that statement so many times growing up.

You see, that marriage was built on adultery—lies, deceit, and lust. Although I thought of all the wonderful things I could do to make my marriage work, I failed to realize this marriage simply would not work because it was not ordained by God. The seeds of disharmony and disobedience had been sown and I was reaping the harvest.

Prior to, and during the marriage, God dealt with me on the seeds that had been sown after separation during my first marriage. There was no peace or joy in my spirit. I began to hear sermons on adultery and being unequally yoked. Unequally yoked means that two people are not on one accord with God; so maybe the husband is saved and the wife is not, or maybe the wife is saved and the husband is not. The heated arguments in this marriage led to my having frequent migraine headaches. I was taking an excessive amount of aspirin to relieve the pain which left me with skin bruises, major hair loss, and an endoscope surgery to locate any ulcers—all due to taking aspirins extensively because of a house divided against itself.

He and I finally separated. My children and I were left living in a house with no gas, which we needed for seven months for heat to stay warm and for cooking. I was drained spiritually, emotionally, mentally, socially, financially, and physically at that point. I was broken, but I was still standing! And I am "STILL STANDING" after so many years later! I knew only God could restore me.

I was one who worried about what "man" had to say. I did not want to feel the shame and guilt of my decision. We often make choices, but we fail to realize all of these choices come with a harvest. The Word of God tells us to choose life or death. Choosing life can bring forth many blessings from God. On the other hand, choosing death can bring forth many curses. (Deuteronomy 30:19). It seems as though I was choosing all the negatives when it came to my life.

In February 2004, pending a divorce, I was living a single life again, with my two children. I was still a little vulnerable, but I was committed to recovery. I was headed toward the road to healing and deliverance! The anointing, wisdom and spiritual gifts had started to be birthed out of me. I had to tell myself no more going from man to man. I had the time to self-examine and evaluate the life I was living and my actions as a result of my thinking. Living a life for God and being a good role model for my children was my first priority. A path of freedom, righteousness, peace, and truth was standing before me – and this is the course I wanted to take!

I can remember how my children had been scarred after years of transitions and because of decisions I had made. This hurt me to the core of my heart. God is still restoring. As I reflect back, I can clearly see how I involved my innocent children in my bad relationships due to poor decisions from the time they entered this world. Because of the choices I made, they had been brought into situations obviously unhealthy for them and me. I have learned that it can truly damage the minds of children when they witness such negative behavior. Children are not really receptive to anyone outside of their biological parents, if all they see year after year is mom and dad. However, we know that over time they will accept what they see, depending on one's character. But, forcing them to accept someone who we chose over them is quite selfish, especially when they have discerned the truth about a person but you do not find out until later.

By now, most of you know that not everyone is fit to be parents. Some questions you should ask include, "Are you and the person you had children with effective parents? Are you the kind of parents that can raise mentally, emotionally, socially, spiritually healthy children by example?" It is time to do a reality check. The truth is there have been times when I felt that I was not being a good mother. I felt quite unfit. My children and I were in environments that involved negative behavior daily because I was trying to change men that did not want to change and searching for love impatiently in all the wrong places. My children were depending on me to choose a better environment.

My children witnessed their mom arguing with these men for various reasons, and then I tried to cover it up with smiles even though I was truly hurting. And most of the arguments involved change. It is one thing when you have received your purpose to help bring about change in a person's life. It is another matter to try and force change, and to make someone more suited for our reasons. This is out of order. This is selfish. But, if I have gained anything out of my bad relationship/marriage choices, it would be to self-examine and change within because you cannot change another person. As a matter of fact, change can only come from within. Many people are trying to change outwardly first. I challenge you right now to find those things within you that you want to change.

Below are a few questions I want you to think about before I go any further in sharing my journey.

- Have you ever felt unfit as a mother?
- Do you feel that you can do better as a mother?
- Are you subjecting yourself to an unhealthy relationship/marriage that is affecting your innocent children?
- Are you in a cycle now?
- Do you feel your mothering qualities are being challenged?
- Do you feel unworthy?

I ask you to please examine yourself if you answered yes to any of these questions. Your positive response to these questions could be a result of your brokenness. God can fix you. You do not have to feel unworthy anymore. Oftentimes, God will test your character.

As my character was being developed, I felt the Spirit of God moving in my life. I knew and He knew that there was something on the inside of me that represented more than just repeating these negative cycles – and something more than just allowing me to produce more fruit! I knew there had to be more! I knew that I could do all things through Him who strengthens me (Philippians 4:13). You see, even when I was partying, God had me! Even through my bad relationship choices, God had me! I can never forget how much He loves me. I thank Him for not giving up on me. I found out through it all, that He is the only One who can truly love me unconditionally. This is true for you, too. Let me take you back to when I first met Him, and how I learned about my purpose.

PART THREE

I was 12 years old when I first learned of Jesus and His purpose. Well, I guess I should say I was 12 years old when I gained a clearer understanding of who He is. My father would tell us that Jesus had so much power. As I started reading the Bible for myself, I learned that His power was true. Jesus was sent to direct us back to our Heavenly Father. I read about how He healed the broken-hearted, set the captives free, cast out devils, and performed many other miracles. He was the One who took the keys from hell.

Our family would have Bible study in our living room at least once a week, with the exception of those times my father would order my mother to wake us up at 3:00 a.m. or 4:00 a.m. to read the Bible to us. He would share many stories in the Bible of those who had been used by God before Jesus ever walked the earth. He would share the stories of Abraham, Isaac and Jacob. He told us that God is the reason we live, breathe, walk and talk. But one thing my father did in the process of us having those early morning Bible sessions was—cuss at us, while holding the Bible in his hands. I know you are saying, "You have got to be kidding, Yolanda." But, no, I am not kidding! This is real.

My father would call one of our names and ask, "What did I just read?" If we could not repeat the Scripture he had read, we were going to get a whipping. Yes, even if we were too sleepy to focus—well, that included all of us because all of us were too tired at that time of the morning. Mind you, we still had to go to school, after being awakened so early. (*I once said to myself, now how can a man that could expound on the Word of God as he did be so controlling...and cuss with the Bible in his hands?*).

Because of my father's aggressive, dominating approach in teaching us about the Bible, there was a certain fear planted within me that made it difficult for me to even want to even read the Bible. My siblings also felt the same. Since I had been an adult and blessed with a deeper understanding of the Bible, I am not only thankful for His miracle-working power but for the greatest power of all: The power to forgive, nurture, correct and protect. I thank Him for health and strength, and for certain gifts and talents He has bestowed upon me and others—even for the small things that are the big things we often forget or take for granted.

Most of all I pray that more of us will come to develop a relationship with Him and not just be a churchgoer, scripture reader, or verse quoter—that we will come to love ourselves and become sensitive to the needs of others. I can reflect on how there were people when I was in high school that had a handicap. They were different in body, and many of us perceived this as such, but truly we are all spiritual beings who are having a human or physical experience, not the other way around. Now, I say this to express that I now pray for the mind, heart, and spirit of everyone—there is so much that I pray for and thank Him for in realizing that I am truly blessed.

I was taught to pray every night. Even before I accepted Him, I prayed. I would say to myself, "If anybody can create me, then I know they've got me." But as a child I did not know I really had to accept Him. I questioned, "Why anybody wouldn't want to accept Him?" Nonetheless, at one point, it was hard for me to accept Him.

I got saved at the age of 25 and that is when I made the choice to follow Him. I still had faults, and had not yet tasted wholeness, but I learned that He had a plan and purpose for my life. I was created by Him to fulfill my destiny. I joined First Baptist Church, Acipco, under the leadership of the late Pastor Vincent Provitt. I started singing in the choir and serving God. This was a big shift for me, yet a roadmap to my ultimate purpose. I was a baby Christian, but I knew that God wanted to do something awesome in my life that was waiting to be birthed out of me in a season such as now.

Later, I joined Full Gospel Fellowship Church, under the leadership of Pastor Willie L. Brown, Jr. This church was truly geared toward helping to restore those who had been abused on some level. He definitely shared the uncompromising Word of God—he was straight to the point. You were not going to hear a watered down sermon, nor one that made you feel good. Also, he had a way of challenging his members to go to the level that God has for us all. I served as a worship leader and youth praise dance leader for a short time. I was also on the prayer warrior team and I was part of our women's ministry. This was an area of ministry that God tested and developed in me. I had the opportunity to minister to a group of women at our 2005 Annual Women's Conference. Prior to that, I was chosen to share a "Word" during the pastor's anniversary the same year, and then another opportunity prior to that. It felt good to be a part of God's family and to share his Word with others through the different church ministries I was involved in.

In the midst of all this, God had revealed to my former pastor that ministry was definitely in me. It was in 2007 when my purpose was shared through a profound thought—and that still small voice had spoken to me. The small voice shared with me that my purpose is to minister to women through my writing. I was very thankful for a new beginning and a new level!

The Bible makes more sense to me now that I have matured spiritually. I am not only looking at things through my natural eyes but also my spiritual eyes. The life of Jesus was so awesome. Yes, He performed so many miracles. Once I read the Gospels, I learned that He spoke many parables. These were stories that so many of us can relate to today. Even though His disciples walked with Him daily, He could only reveal things to them based on their level of maturity. It is the same way now. As I reflect on my childhood, I can see clearly that learning of Him created a desire in me to now do as Jesus did. What I have also learned is that there are so few doing the work He did.

I often ask myself: *Why are we building bigger buildings? How many people are we attracting because of the physical beauty of the building? How many people are leaving the building because of the spirit inside of the building? Is it the spirit of God? Or is it the spirit of self? How many people are really being taught, verses being entertained? How many people are being healed from their wounds of brokenness?* The bottom line is the number of souls that are truly being saved through our introducing them to God, and teaching them the whole truth? As believers, we must ask ourselves these kinds of questions.

Now what my spirit has truly connected with is the fact that God was one of true benevolence. He loved people. Just as God sent Jesus to do a mighty work and fulfill His purpose, He has also sent us to do greater works. Even Jesus told His disciples they will do greater works than He had done just before His death, resurrection, and return home to be with our Father to watch, lead and guide us in our work.

But just like I heard of Jesus, I would hear stories of an enemy—the kind of enemy that is common to all of us—and that is Satan. You know the one who causes the chaos and brings many adverse circumstances in our lives. Yes, he does. You may even know him as the devil, an adversary and the prince of the air. Satan is just the plan old evil one.

When I was a child I would often be attacked by spirits, but I did not know why. I would question my mother and father about the many attacks that I was experiencing, being so young. Literally, there would be times that I could not even move my body. As I grew older, I would hear stories of how Satan knows your purpose before you ever thought about it, and he came to steal, kill and destroy our lives. I have learned that our life here on earth is all about purpose. It is about knowing and fulfilling our purpose whether we realize that or not. I have also learned that Satan will do whatever he can to take control of your mind and hinder you from fulfilling your ultimate purpose.

Speaking of purpose, it was my purpose that the enemy started attacking when I was young, like some of you, trying to block what God has intended. Seemingly, the things I said I would never subject myself to are the exact things the enemy played on—and has always played on. It seems as though he scoped me out as a child, maybe you, too. Okay, let me put it in another way. Sadly, the very things I observed as a child, which was contrary to God's purpose in and for the family, were those very things used as devices to keep me in prison in a world of selfishness rather than service.

You may ask yourself what I mean by this. Well, can you think of times when you observed something in your childhood, whether it was mental or physical abuse that your parents went through and you said that you would never go through it or at least you hoped you would not have to face anything that is so devastating to the human mind? But now, you have found yourself facing the very thing you said that you did not want to go through. In other words, you feared. Now what you have feared has come upon you because you were either thinking it would happen to you or you spoke it into existence. The power of the tongue is a strong weapon. I have learned that you can definitely invite unwanted things in your life, even in your thoughts. Job warned us against that. He proved that we should focus more on the positive things we do want according to God's will rather than for what we do not want. We will always invite those things in our lives that we concentrate on most.

How does fear come about? Just like faith comes by hearing, fear comes by hearing—hearing over and over in your mind—that is where it starts. Can you remember how your mother or father would put that fear in you? Well, this was the kind of fear that if I did something wrong, I knew that it was automatically a whipping, even before they found out about what I did. They would say things like, "You'd better not go with him or her, or the dishes better be washed by the time I get home." Okay, when I did things contrary to their rules—that was my butt.

As I stated before, faith comes by hearing. Well, I believe fear works just the same, even now. I have heard spiritual leaders teach on fearing this enemy called Satan. Since I have studied and know for myself that there is an Almighty God, our Father, with all power, I do not want to even think about the enemy. In Matthew 18:18 we read, "Verily I say unto you, whatsoever ye shall bind on earth shall be bound in heaven: and whatsoever ye shall loose on earth shall be loosed in heaven." So that means I can loose power, healing, deliverance and freedom over my situation. And I do not even have to entertain Satan at all. My goal is strictly pleasing my Father. I believe if I continue to focus on God, I will not have any time to invite the enemy in my life—ever. I will be about my Father's business, as Jesus was, which He stated many times.

After reading Job's story mentioned in the Bible, I learned that everything he feared came upon him. Now as I relate Job's story to mine, I can clearly see, at one point in my life, what I most feared came upon me too, especially as it relates to the many transitional relationships. I found myself losing everything I had as a result of my thinking and speaking, which led to bad relationship choices, coupled with my overall brokenness. When you are taught how to fear you begin to look for negative things to happen. Guess what? They will happen, as long as you fear. Now, I am not saying that we do not have an enemy, but we should think about and focus on our Heavenly Father, and we will find that He will be the center of our situations. Do not invite Satan in your life through fear, like I did.

I was scarred as a child. And the broken child that once lived in me for many, many years has just recently been healed through confession, meditation, prayer, seeking, faith and love. I was a child that missed some of the important things that I needed to be an effective, healthy-minded and well-balanced adult, especially concerning dating.

Think about what I just mentioned earlier regarding the enemy gripping hold to something—that broken child and taking her to a place she does not desire to go. For me, that was subjecting myself to men who seemed to have had some of the characteristics {dominate, angry, etc} of my father. As I observed my parents' marriage, I thought relationships should be based on how their relationship was.

I wanted to prevent having someone like my father, but I found myself attracting men who were in essence like my father. They were broken too. I have come to know that it is not uncommon to live by what you observe as a child. It is rather easy to accept the things that are unacceptable, because in your little innocent mind you think it is all right. I grew determined not to give the enemy any place in my life.

Before I end my story, I want to share with you how I was delivered me from the very thing that had me bound for a long time (transitioning from man to man). And seemingly the weakness I had been yielding to is what He used to bring deliverance—and that is a man.

One day, I met a minister, who happens to be my dear friend. I opened up the line of communication with him. He said that God gave him a vision that a woman would come into his life and that his purpose was for us to help each other to get to the next level. Shortly after having that vision, he said that he was led to the church I was a member of, and he knew at a youth ministry meeting that I was that young lady, because God had shown him. He said that it was something about the presence in the room. At first, I did not initially connect with the reasons for him coming into my life, but as time progressed, I began to see the scope of it.

After communicating with him for the first time, he was able to identify with my brokenness. He stated that, "God wants to deliver you from people, and I can tell that you have been emotionally wounded." I was amazed that he knew that, even before I shared my story. That is the kind of God we serve. You see, He knows who, when, why and how to deliver you from the very thing that you have so freely given yourself to time after time. Again, it was not easy to accept the reasons for him coming into my life. Why? Because coming out of many transitions, this was a comfort zone. So my thoughts of him being the one for me is what was running through my mind.

Now, as friends, we have had our challenges too, those that forced me out of my comfort zone—what I was used to doing. And those that forced him out of his comfort zone. I can truly say boldly that our friendship has been fruitful. God allowed both of us to be used by Him to bring deliverance in each other's lives.

I have learned that when you desire a relationship with every man you meet (even if he is no good for you)—to meet a man who clearly sees that you have been emotionally wounded, and rejects the fact that you want to pursue a relationship because it is about God, is an awesome thing. I needed to realize that every man that came into my life was not going to be the man God has for me—my husband. Why try to make it be? I can even remember him saying, in the first stages of our friendship, "Yo, growing pains don't always feel good."

I must admit, I was still struggling with being patient—I was a "right now" woman. You see, relationship dependency was the "norm." But I needed to practice patience and wait on God to move in every part of my life, even concerning a mate. God was trying to heal me emotionally. You and I really need to see if a man that comes into our life is our assignment, or if we are his assignment. I can truly say that we were both each other's assignment. What I mean by this is that some people will come into your life and they will be assigned to carry out a certain task (encourage you; listen to you...be a blessing to you). He told me over and over again, "Yo, you need to be by yourself." We have known each other for years, and we have gone through many fiery trials together; been on the battlefield fighting for each other. Standing on the Word of God and staying focused is how we have made it through the trials in that season of my life. Ladies, we need to know if a man we meet is just coming into our life to cause us harm or to be of any "help." This is where trusting God, patience, and discernment come into play.

Speaking of discernment, well, it was during the challenging times of our friendship when a church-going man had planted the first seeds of a later harvest that proved to be a harvest in God's way and in my way. I was decreasing so that God could increase more in having His way.

You did not catch that, did you? I said, "A church-going man!" He said that the anointing is what attracted him to me. Yet, he was vulnerable (I was too), but mentioned that he had a crush on me. After a few conversations, he said that I was his wife. How many times have I heard that? But when you are vulnerable, it will make you feel things you really do not feel, and accept things that are untrue. Now both of our thoughts were heading in the same direction, but because of the shield that God had around me, and the deliverance He was trying to bring in my life, the relationship was not able to move beyond two months. In other words, it had ended before it even got started. Later, the man got married. Now, how could I have possibly been his wife? It worked out just fine because God knows how to stop and block any emotional setups that the enemy is trying to trap you in. The cycle definitely has to be broken.

Let me share a word of wisdom with you—PATIENCE. Most of you hear the word *church*—oh, he goes to church—and nearly lose your minds. And believe me, I was one of them. There are a great number of women who fall in love with the idea of a man going to church, instead of the idea of church being in the man, in his heart. That seems to be the biggest trick the enemy has used on us and is still using, especially, if your focus is moving in the direction of marriage or just having a man. It does not always have to be something negative about that man, but it has more to do with what God is trying to do in your life. He wants to bring you to a place of wholeness in your "singleness." Be patient and just wait.

First of all, can you see how a distraction can come in the midst of your deliverance taking place? Just think about it! God is trying to bring deliverance in your life, but here comes that common enemy we all share. At moments like that you really need to stay focused. I had to be strong as I began to move forward.

At the beginning of this new level, I began to read more and more truth-based books. There were many books that helped me, such as, *Why? Because You Are Anointed* written by T.D. Jakes! *8 Ways to Overcome Adversity* written by Joyce Meyer! *Seduction Exposed* written by Dr. Greenwald! *Expect the Extraordinary* written by Jerry Savella! *My Spiritual Inheritance* written by Juanita Bynum! I began thinking in the direction God was trying to take me. I can truly say all of these books and more helped me to gain the knowledge and understanding I was craving. This was really important because I knew that I needed both of them, along with wisdom to make better decisions.

I was determined not to get involved in another relationship until God was ready to unite me with "**the** man" He desires for me—for the purpose of marriage and ministry. Falling in love with God was all I needed. I began to see that it was more about my relationship with Him than anything else. Since then, I have been able to experience all of His goodness and glory. I can say that I was set free from the agony of unfruitful relationships.

It was only because of His grace and mercy that I did not lose my mind. You see, I basically had my own agenda. I was a broken vessel, searching for love—impatiently. I am now convinced that if I just wait on God, everything will be all right.

Let us move on. Do you remember me mentioning how our friendship produced much fruit? Well, I am pleased to share how God can position a willing vessel to play a role in growth, healing, wholeness as he did. Here is my testimony.

FROM TRIALS TO TRIUMPH

I started graduate school on August 26, 2005, about three years after I gained my bachelor's degree in business administration. There were several challenging circumstances leading up to this point. I "believed" that God was bigger than these storms and could bring me out with commitment, determination, and unwavering Faith. I came to "know" during my journey through school, which was accentuated when my name was called, and I reached out, wearing a cap and gown, only to receive the by-product of all that God has purposed for my life.

The one thing to be understood without a doubt is that it is not about me. It is all about God reaching His people to transform areas of their lives, which He has offered through His divine promises. I am not confused about that, and I know that God is not the author of confusion. Now, confusion, from the very beginning of my decision could have prevailed as the enemy of the Heavenly Father's plan for my life, in this season of my life.

God is not a peace-breaker but instead He is a peacemaker. The peace I enjoyed surrounding the decision to enroll in graduate school which was centered upon positive reasons, was immediately attacked by those you would least expect with negative reasons of why I should not go back, why I did not "need" to go back, and why my decision was ill-timed. It is amazing what we can learn about others and ourselves when we share our hopes, dreams, goals, or plans. What I have learned is to remain prayerful and careful with whom I share high-impact matters with.

Imagine the excitement! I had beaten tremendous odds and overcame many obstacles to go from a teenage mother to giving birth to a second child by age 23, experienced two marriages, and despite a life of mental and emotional abuse, I still preserved and gained a bachelor's degree with a desire to climb higher. I wanted to "be all that I could be." I wanted to make a better life for me and my children. I wanted to secure the finances to offer them (and others), the much needed support I did not have. I shared all of these goals and dreams with church folk, family, and friends who smiled in my face and spoke words of support while secretly they spoke among each other against me.

Yes, I heard it all directly and indirectly from so many who said, "How is she going to go back to school with two children to raise?" to "God is not telling you to go back to school" to "Why is she going back to school?" One thing I can truly say is a friend truly sticks closer than a brother or sister, and I am thankful for my true friends who want more out of life both recognizing and encouraging me to do the same. I also thank God for those special brothers and sisters among all my siblings who truly are friends. There are many dream stealers in our lives and Judases (the one who betrayed Jesus) who walk with us, yet do not walk in agreement with us. This is something my good friend, Minister Vince Collins, would repeatedly share. I finally got it! He would often ask, "Why do you think Jesus admonished go and tell no man?" Today I can answer, but there is a blessed paradox in this matter. Before I offer this answer there is more.

God will always place in our lives great people in times of great need. On some level I had been in a place of great need whether it was recognized at the time or not, seemingly all my life. Yet, this was a time I knew without a doubt that I was in a fight without hands, with few "hands" reaching out to help in any form. When I was wrestling with the seeds of thought that had been planted in my mind concerning "God telling me to go back to school," I had the prayers and encouragement of my friend and sister in Christ, Phyllis. I also had the full support of my longtime friends, classmates, and sisters in Christ, Anita and Shundala; and my sister Tonya. However, it was that special God-infused wisdom, knowledge, and understanding of Phyllis and Vince that really pushed me forward.

I can remember the prayers, words of wisdom, and the scriptures Phyllis shared with me. Vince, on the other hand, had a way of challenging my thoughts in a way that I truly give God the glory for. I can remember much of what he shared in our many conversations. Over and over he would say, "Yo, you have always been there for those that have not been there for you. You have a heart, mind and soul to be a blessing to so many people. You've given of your time and finances to help others. You've given of your mental and emotional resources to a fault. You place seemingly so much above your own happiness. You've been blessed with wisdom, knowledge, and understanding." He asked, "Could it be that God is about to add greatly to your understanding?"

What I most remember him saying is, "God will not hinder His own agenda." Moses was called (purposed) to do a great work. God told him that He wanted him to deliver the children of Israel out of bondage, but things did not happen the way, or as soon as, Moses thought they should. Things did not happen easily. Moses did not achieve immediate success but it did not affect the outcome. He initially reached for every excuse possible. He told God that he could not do it because of his speech impediment. God answered by giving him someone to go with him, Aaron. The outcome was successful. There were lessons learned and taught during the process. The issue was process." (More information on Moses is available in the book of Exodus).

This one thing I do know: What God says about something is all that matters! Yet, when your desire is strong and your finances are weak and absolutely necessary to get you to the next level in your purpose, responding as Moses did is easy. Now, as I sat taking the Miller Analogies Test both the bitter and sweet leading up to this point came to mind. Yes, the money came through for me, and with only one day before classes started, there I was seated in a seat of faith and trusting God. Not only did I past this test, absolutely necessary to enroll in class, I knew that I had passed certain other of life's tests as well. What Vince had been telling me all along is something that I had believed but came to "know." "There is no problem that exists outside of our own heads. It is how we respond that matters most." This was not only a season of challenge it was a season of growth and change. Grad school, here I come!! August 25, 2006, will always be remembered as a day of victory against all odds!

The very next day I found myself at Troy University in Montgomery, Alabama, in an atmosphere of stress and strain because of a lengthy registration process. I arrived around 4:00 p.m. that evening.

My first class session was scheduled for 7:00 p.m. There I was among students who voiced their opinions about registration while I fought to focus on my journey to be there and give thanks. At this time, I met a young lady that would be God's wink of approval for one of the many reasons for my being there, and a symbolic voice that silenced all of the negative comments at my announcement of going to grad school.

This young lady and I struck up conversation amid the many conversations lending to the registration pandemonium. I immediately recognized her demeanor—that look in her eyes and facial expressions did more than suggest frustration with the registration process. She began to freely share her discontentment in the matter, but I was able to discern there was more going on with her. She shared how she wanted to give up on even trying to complete the process because things were so hectic that night. Patiently, I began to respond and encourage her. The first words out of my mouth were, "You can do all things through Christ who strengthens you." I then encouraged her to read that particular verse (Philippians 4:13) whenever she felt like giving up.

I thank God and I am both honored and humbled that she could open up about her frustrations. As we talked, I could feel the deeply rooted pain. She shared enough for God to reveal her mental and emotional brokenness. What I have learned over the years in my journey from a victim of brokenness on the road to wholeness is that mental and emotional brokenness is synonymous to the lack of spiritual wholeness. No amount of smiles, even nonchalant behavior, can cover up the truth. The spirit of God will find us out. I was found out once upon a time, and I am thankful for this. I sincerely believe that this young lady is also thankful.

Later, as we shared breakfast one Saturday morning, I learned she was dealing with troubles in her marriage. I listened to her carefully and I was blessed to share with her from a standpoint of having been an over-comer in many of the very areas she spoke about. We prayed and until this day, I am thankful to the Heavenly Father for meeting her. I learned a lot from this opportunity to minister to her. One, she admitted that she was thankful for God placing me on her path.

The thanks she gave me, was all about God. As she thanked me for reminding her of that special message to her heart, mind, and soul found in Philippians 4:13 a couple of weeks later, God was using her to give me what He used me to give her, "You can do all things through Christ who strengthens you." I had also shared with her some of the particulars of the struggles I had faced. At that time, I simply wanted her to know that she was not alone and that God had us both. In some small way my hope was that she could find strength in knowing that I had multiple peace-threatening issues that I was determined to stand up against and win. She was there to minister back to me.

Only God knows how much I needed those same encouraging words, and only He knows how much I needed that $50 seed she planted in my hand one morning before class. Let me share this, when her name was called to receive the degree, I could not help but think of both our journeys from the beginning up to that very moment. She is now happy and free, doing well and gainfully employed.

Although we have not spoken since we both graduated, I continue to speak blessings on her life and thank God for the opportunity to make a difference. There is a passage of scripture that I am reminded of when I think of her and others that God allowed me to minister to while in school, Truly God, the Shepherd will leave ninety-nine sheep just to save the one. (Matthew 18:12-14). I am particularly grateful that the Shepherd used me. God proved that not only was it His will for me to get in school, He helped me to take something out of the experience. That is the truth in knowing that all the negative talk surrounding my going to school can be answered in God placing me right where He wanted me to be. What God says is all that matters.

Remember I mentioned how much I thanked God and her for coming to me weeks later to thank me for the encouraging scripture? There is a reason. Actually, there are several reasons that started just as I started school.

Shortly after I started grad school, the company I had worked for just over two years was bought out. Before the acquisition, I had enjoyed somewhat of a financial good-health status. With base pay and monthly bonuses and incentives, there was more than enough to take care of my family, bless others in need of a little help, and have money left over. That is to say, I was blessed not to live pay check to pay check. The buy-out and transition was nothing shy of financially, mentally, and emotionally draining. Spiritually, I was fighting even harder than I was leading up to getting in school. I realized that God was doing something great in my life, and there is sunshine on the other side. Joy comes in the morning, yet I definitely felt the reality of a long night.

First, just before the transition that robbed me of my financial stability there was the issue of car repairs that took about $1,500 out of my household and set me back. That was one of the main reasons I was setback and was short on cash to take the pre-grad school test mentioned earlier. Why not tell it all? Also I was setback by loaning a friend some money for car repairs that they committed to pay for on my good name—it never happened. I was stuck with the $400 bill and got slightly behind on rent and other obligations. I thank God for Vince's contribution at that time. The price we pay for emotions and poor choices can affect us when money is needed to take advantage of good choices requiring money. This taught me to truly wait on God and not be in denial about the signs.

Well, there was one sign that was inescapable. This was the sign that had financial struggle and unhappiness written all over it after the transition. I realize that I'm sharing all this in an almost rambling fashion. Hopefully, you are still with me. There is much more.

Okay, ladies, one thing that resulted from this transition was a promotion to a management position. This new position paid well, very well, but I, Yolanda, was not getting paid. Of course, this was not known at the time I accepted the position. Initially, I thought the pay increase would have filled the gap with respect to the loss of the incentive pay received prior to the acquisition. But guess what? This never happened.

I was doing the work of a manager, had the responsibilities of a manager, had a promotion as a manager complete with company memos to fellow employees, but the pay of a team leader. As a matter of fact, the more I reflect on all of the congratulations received, with well wishes ringing in my ears the more furious I would become. I knew the pay was low. The stress and responsibilities were high. Nonetheless, I kept pressing on. I performed as though I was being honored for my bachelor's degree and was being paid accordingly. That is, until I could not take it anymore. You would be surprised what much prayer and a little research can do for validating that gut feeling of truth being withheld.

The deal was that I was being used for my degree and talents to cover for a manager without a degree or the experience that this position called for. In sum, I was helping to earn her paycheck. When I think about the various protocols I developed for the department and other suggestions I had made in the best interest of all involved, it still kind of rubs me the wrong way to know that these things were often discounted on the front end, and played up on the back end as the doings of management. Of course, by now you know that management did not include me. After months of unfair wages and treatment, I learned more from the employees of the company that took over. I could see that there was no one to turn to within our local office. I forwarded my concern to corporate, and they made a mess of it all.

What is really interesting is that prior to all this madness on the job, I had a dream revealing the spiritual nature of what I would soon experience on the job. As things started to unfold I knew it was time for me to go. Most of us never consider the spirituality of the people who employ us. Truly, we need to hold this in high account. Most of my problems stemmed from a minister's wife—a church going woman who didn't seem to have church inside of her heart. Yes. What is in your heart will definitely come out. It will be shown through your actions, and that is a truth.

I have learned on my journey that there are many part-time believers and Christians. Many call Jesus' name on Sunday, and they walk in love, too. Well, at least, it seems like it, but from Monday through Saturday, the light within them is dim. One thing that is certain is that those who treat others unfairly based on religion, race, color, age, sex, and call themselves children of God need to search their hearts for truth. Ask yourself this question, "Am I walking in love? Can I walk in love, even when I'm mistreated?"

Through all the humiliation of being told my degree did not even matter—and being used and drained mentally and emotionally—God gave me the strength to endure. I thanked Him much then and even now in looking back. Proverbs 29:2 tells of a truth that cannot be disputed, "When the righteous are in authority the people rejoice: but when the wicked beareth rule the people mourn" (KJV). There are no limits. This can apply to your job, home, church—anywhere an authoritative position is being held.

One of the greatest lessons learned from this experience is God's people have no business working in a business (even church) that does not honor God's people and does not uphold the highest level of integrity, despite what the brochures say. We must always take a stand for what's right even when it hurts. There are certain situations that can bless us for a season, yet not intended for us to get complacent. I was in total mourning, but I knew He had a plan for my life. I knew that I had to stand in faith because the wicked selfishly didn't see the harm they were doing and causing; however, it was all a blessing for me. My time was almost up, and I had to depend on Him for direction. I had a deep feeling in my soul there was work for me to do elsewhere.

Now all of this was going on during my first semester. There was trouble on every side it seemed. My income did not permit me to drive more than 200 miles round trip to school twice a week (on the weekends) and cover hotel costs. The money was not there and this is reality. I tried hard not to drift into a complaining mode. I was in the process of being delivered from complaining. He had placed someone in my life to help in this area, but nonetheless, money was short and I did have concerns. In the midst of it all came a ray of hope each and every week. God made a way every time without fail. Truly it is impossible for Him to fail any of us.

With all this chaos, I started contemplating, meditating, and seeking God for direction. I needed Him to make it plain to me as to whether or not my time had expired in faithfully serving an employer that did not honor or respect me, along with countless others over the years. An eight-to-five job can seem like eternal torment when you are unhappy in any situation, having done all you know to do to make things better with others involved not showing any interest to commit to positive change. I did not want to make an emotional decision. This is a matter placed in God's hands and left there.

Finally, I gained peace in the direction I needed to go. The decision was followed by a dream I had one night in which all I could remember was the chapter and verse number of a scripture without the name of the book from which it was taken. What I got was 115:3. When I awoke, immediately my thoughts fell on the book of Psalm. I read all of Psalm 115. After meditating day and night on this, I had much peace in knowing it was time for me to leave this place. A few days later, I put in my two-week notice and I resigned from this position. However, I was asked to go ahead and leave after one week. I was hurt, but I was paid for those two weeks. God is good.

Initially, I told only those close to me of my decision to leave, but it was only a matter of time before the word got out. There was negativity surrounding this decision. There will be those in your life that will talk against you simply because they have vocal cords. One thing's for certain, those who are locked into looking at things with their natural eyes only and hearing things with their natural ears cannot possibly discern what is spiritually being done.

I always had a certain assurance. Strangely, I was not worried. I would ask God to deliver me mentally and emotionally. See, I believe this was one of the reasons that Vince had come into my life. He had recognized my need to gain freedom from being bound to the thoughts of others. I must admit, I was one that worried about what people had to say. It was during this time that things started to make more than sense. God was giving me a glimpse of what He was doing and making happen in the spirit realm.

This move was "out of the norm" for most people. The very thing that most people fear is losing their income. My family, as well as others, did not understand that I was gaining God's outcome. We all know that earning a living is important in order to take care of our families.

What God was doing was setting me up to experience the understanding that He was in the process of adding more life to my living and shifting my thoughts—from a job being the only way to support my family to leaning and depending on Him as my sole provider. This is with or without employment. It is God who gives us the ability to get wealth (Deuteronomy 26). He provides for His people based on their purpose according to His will. It is not a matter of 'want' when we submit ourselves to God and answer the call to service—His service. God is responsible for every person, place, or thing that belongs to Him.

Don't get me wrong, we should work if we are able bodied. The thing is, most people depend on their jobs and look to their employers for their livelihood. Too often we rely on college degrees, networking, experience, or a combination of all. As for me, I had grown to know that none of this means anything if there is something specific God wants you to do.

God has never forsaken me. Through some of the biggest crisis in my life, and the life of my children, He has been right there. In the good times He was there, too. I give Him thanks during the good and bad times. God is faithful. The more I realized this, the more my desire grows to please Him and become more willing and obedient in the smallest of matters. God will supply our needs and allow the supply to get scarce in order for us to recognize Him as the source of our supply. And no matter the beginning, the end is victorious. There is a process. I have learned to appreciate the process.

It was now time for the second semester to begin. I no longer had a job, and I was not sure of all the details of how I was going to make it but certain with total faith. With no prospects for employment and low to no money most of the time, I, as well as my decision, was becoming suspect. You might be asking, "Girl, why on earth did you quit your job?" If this comes to mind your thoughts are not alone. Many people asked this question, but of course I can only give one answer. Regardless of what things looked like on the surface I trusted God totally. Do you remember my sharing the conversation with Minister Vince in which he ministered to me about Moses being called to do something that did not immediately go as he may have thought, and all those lessons Moses had to learn and the strength he had to gain from it all? Well, this story had Yolanda written all over it. And it is very real to me to this day.

The question of how was I going to get back and forth to school at this point were followed by more insulting questions and comments than the going-back-to-school issue did. Now, as God was taking me to a higher level in Him mentally, emotionally, and spiritually don't think that the enemy did not seize the opportunity to launch an all out attack to judge, criticize, scandalize, and defame my character. And he used as many people as he could. It's almost as though people had become willing vessels for the enemy to beat up on me.

Oh, I heard it all, "You need to get another job," "You've got two children to take care of," "You're a fool," "You're going to lose your apartment," "God wouldn't have told you to quit your job to struggle," "I'm not going to help you with money because you're able to work," "You can't pay back any money if you borrow any because you don't have a job." But you know what? Phyllis, Anita, Vince, and my sister Tonya were right there with prayer, encouragement, and just speaking life into my situation. Needless to say, I pressed on.

Now one of the highlights of all this was explaining the situation to my children. Although my son was only nine years old at the time, his response was as much a blessing as those five close ministering angels that I have mentioned repeatedly. He is wise beyond his years; he would pray and encourage me, and this blessed me deeply. My daughter was supportive in her own way yet not as vocal. See, the years of transition had taken a toll on our relationship at that time, nonetheless, I believed that this new place God was taking me would bless my household. The blessing was that my children truly understood as best they could, my passion to allow God to fully lead us. And this He has. It doesn't mean we didn't face challenges, but we also experience some positive changes in the midst of the storms.

I was holding on by faith as never before—still holding on to my joy! Still praying! Still loving! Still caring! Still encouraging! Still laying hands on the sick! Still doing spiritual warfare on behalf of others! I was not going to be defeated. I began to notice that although people were speaking more negative now than in the past I was at peace. I could feel the growth of being delivered from people more and more. The enemy thought he had me. Satan thought that if enough negative energy surrounded me that I would give up and give in. Oh no! Even when things did not look good, I moved forward with total faith and trust in God.

And, oh yes, I continued to press my way back and forth to school. Well, during the third semester with three classes left and 10 semester hours, three days before midterm exams—my car was repossessed. I will never forget my son's reaction to this incident. He shouted to the top of his voice that someone was taking the car as I studied for the exam. He was very upset. I could see the concern in his eyes. He asked, "Mom, how are you going to get around?" and "How are you going to get to school?" I assured him that everything would turn out favorably. I explained that God would make a way for me to get around and back and forth to school. I told him that we would get another car. I explained that God allows certain things to happen in order to move us closer to Him and to make room for what He ultimately has in store.

Since that night God has delivered on everything that I shared with my son. I was blessed to get to school, and I was blessed to get a car in February 2007. It took some time to get a car, but I got a better car than my old 2000 Mazda. God is good!

Now, I was rather upset but still managed to hold on strong. Do not think for one moment that tears were not shed that night. Oh, yes, many tears fell. For some reason it was hard to digest the reality of what my son had witnessed. Likewise, it was hard to digest his reaction to it all. I began to pray and cry out to God. Finally, I said to my Heavenly Father, "Not my will but your will be done." I realized that I had to keep myself composed. I simply could not allow myself to become an emotional wreck no matter what. I had a test to prepare for that coming Friday, two days away. I had to find the strength to stay focused.

God always has a ram in the bush. This means that He will always provide. And He did just that. He had positioned my friend, Minister Vince, to be available and a willing vessel in that season. After explaining what had happened, I can remember him saying "Yo, you know I'm there for you." He drove me to school so that I could take my midterm for my financial analysis class. He waited patiently in his car. He would be praying for me, reading, and working on business ideas. He made a commitment to help me out from that moment on. He waited patiently from 5:00 p.m. to 9:00 p.m. for my Friday class and from 8:00 a.m. to 5:00 p.m. for my Saturday class. God is better than good all the time.

I was really nervous after taking the test. A few days later, the results were in. I did not pass the midterm test, but I remained positive. I stood on faith. I kept the voice of my conscience positive. I declared within myself that I would graduate on time. I prayed. Determined to press my way through, I immediately emailed my instructor to find out the score I needed on the final exam to pass the class. He sent an email reply with the necessary score. I had a new target. There was no doubt that I would achieve that score—with God's help. It is amazing how when we focus on something of high positive value in the midst of a storm we often forget we are even in a storm. Or at least, the storm loses its grip on us.

While my thoughts, efforts, and energies were concentrated on this new objective, certain of my circumstances got worse. The heat was turned up a notch. There is no doubt that Satan's furnace was blazing, yet the Potter's oven was heated also. On one hand there appeared to be a trap growing bigger; and on the other hand God was preparing the ingredients for triumph.

A few weeks had passed. Now it was time for my final exam in my most challenging class. As I approached this date, I found myself giving God thanks that this exam was scheduled on a different date than the exam previously mentioned. Now, I was just finishing up a major research project that was assigned in groups of two to four. The score from this coupled with the exam score would tell the story. While optimistically preparing for the test, I received an eviction notice. On the week of the exam my thoughts were forced upon the idea that my children and I could be soon without a home, with no money and no place to go. About this time, I spoke with my good friend, Anita, who immediately opened her doors to my children and me. I thanked her, but I was not ready to give in so easily.

    I prayed and simply focused on a positive outcome. I approached my landlord with a plea for an extension to come up with the money. I had explained my circumstances. Extension granted! I went "to work" trying to get help. I tried my family. Well, there was sensitivity from a couple of my siblings who had the heart to help but did not have the means. Yes, and this does include doors being slammed on me that were opened to others in their season of challenge. I had been there for some even during several seasons of trial. I respect that we all have our immediate families to provide for. I respect this. Over the years I have needed some help and was blessed by the kindness of many. The thing is that when you know someone has it—and would gladly give it to others in the same situation—this can be hurtful and frustrating.

    Well, I tried the friends mentioned throughout this book. Seemingly everyone was being financially challenged at this time. I do not say this in sarcasm, I mean literally. Up to this season my closest friends were OK financially, but they were having challenges at this time. I received a lot of encouragement and as much help as each could offer. This still means a lot. I can remember calling Vince after we had not spoken in a couple of months when I was first coming into this season and told him I needed a certain amount of money to make ends meet. He went over and beyond. He did not question me at all. He simply asked, "Yo, when do you need it?" I answered, "As soon as possible." He had just gotten back from a business trip and was tired. I could hear it in his voice. Yet, the last thing he said before arriving about 30 minutes later was, "I'm on the way!"

    My friend, Phyllis, had the heart, but no money; she was in need too. Not long before this, Anita gave me close to $100 she had intended to put in church. Unlike the majority, she recognized she could meet a need and be a blessing without feeling guilty for not giving to the church. Besides, she said "something" had told her to hold on to it. This happened in advance of my calling her. So when I asked, she gave it. This reminded me of how Jesus addressed the religious minds of His day concerning helping their parents (this could be a neighbor or stranger) in need. The problem Jesus saw was that people were overlooking the needs of their loved ones [then] to give to the church, for the church to do [later, if at all, even if you are a tither] what they had means but not the heart to do. This is true for some churches, but not all. Obviously, benevolence seems of the least importance, among too many Christians and churches. So often, we say to those who have "a right now need" the money we have is Corban! Corban is a gift to God. Yet, Jesus wanted them to see that it was useless to offer a gift to God, thinking this was righteous, while overlooking the needs of their parents. This is totally contrary to God's desire for us to serve one another. (Mark 7:6-13). This brings me to the next place I turned for help.

    I cried out to God, but the answer did not come immediately. But one day on my lunch break while working a temporary job I had just been assigned to, the answer came—churches. I was excited. I gave honor and praise to God for just the thought. I mentioned it to Vince when he came to pick me up from work. He looked at me and said in his heavy voice, "I wrote some churches on your behalf weeks ago with no responses. I even listed character references for you. I didn't tell you because I didn't want you to know anything about it nor did I want those I listed as references to know. I've just been praying and waiting." I remained optimistic. I gave God thanks. A letter was drafted. Letters were sent to a significant number of larger churches (mega-churches and first-stage mega-churches) as well as others in Birmingham and Huntsville, Alabama.

    What I got was a wake-up call. It was God who sounded the alarm. I was blessed to receive a call from one church, followed by two Wal-Mart gift cards. I was thankful. Gift cards were not exactly what I had been seeking God for, but I was most appreciative and put it to good use.

    The second response came from a church that sent a letter that I will never forget. What I most remember were the words—"your circumstances are not uncommon to man, and we will pray for you." My initial thought was, "And I am sure your response in times like this is not uncommon to man either, and I will pray for you." I was not bitter, just shocked. Nonetheless, I was sincerely blessed by both responses. I was blessed just as much by those not responding. Of course, this truth took a while to arrive at, but I eventually got there. Maybe, I should have sent them to the smaller churches. What do you think? After a short time, Vince said, "God takes care of His own." He mentioned my good heart, desire to serve God and others, and live a life of obedience...he expressed his belief that He had something in mind. He truly believed that He was setting me up for a blessing so big that all of these challenges were needed. They were a part of something awesome, but it was all about Him.

Nothing seemed to work. I attached the eviction notice, my impending car repossession notice, even the car repair receipt that was instrumental in the turn-around in finances. I was going to work every day but it seemed to be barely working. The temp job I was working was about 15 miles to 20 miles from my apartment. My apartment was about 20 miles from Vince's house. This was one way. Because he was working, I had to wait for him to pick me up after work. I was only working 25 hours to 30 hours per week at $10 an hour, but I was grateful. I was feeding my children and paying to get from point A to point B, most of the time. I knew this trouble would not last; it was just a short season.

Time had passed and it was now July. The weather was hot. The heat was on in my life and it was about to get hotter. It was July 21, 2006, the scheduled date for my management test. I entered the class after more than 40 hours of study over a two-week period. The room held just over 20 students. It was filled with negative energy—negative energy, due to such a high level of stress. I was not the only student concerned about this test. For me, however, I had to pass this test in order to graduate on time, and I had the shakiness to prove it. The negative vibes seemed to just zap the little bit of confidence that I was holding on to for dear life, and my energy.

It took two weeks to get the test results. I received the results of my management exam on the day of the final exam in my financial analysis class. The moment of truth had arrived. There was no passing grade to get excited about—I had not passed. The best part about this ordeal was the fact that I was able to take this test without the added pressure of knowing I had not passed the financial analysis class. Once more I could feel mental, emotional, and spiritual growth. In some strange way I was relieved. My thoughts were positive. Faith was truly carrying me, and my prayers worked! My management instructor gave students the opportunity to perform one more analysis. You remember my sharing that a certain test score was needed to pass? We will later see what the result was.

The financial analysis test was taken. The management class results had been revealed. A bonus project had been assigned. My thoughts were moving in so many directions. My faith was strong, yet reality struck. I was headed back to Birmingham in the car with classmate/project partner. We had worked together on several projects in management class all year. Only, she had done enough to pass the class, I, on the other hand was dealing with the reality of her absence on that "blessed" bonus project that I so desperately needed in order to "walk" in December.

The pressure was on. The financial analysis instructor informed us the scores would be posted on the school's computer blackboard at 10:00 p.m. that very evening. Based on his proven track record of promptness, I knew he would deliver. My concern was "what" would be delivered. I was a little nervous but still standing! Still praying! Still holding on to God's unchanging hand!

I chose to go to bed. I did not have access to a computer to get the grade, so I was forced to wait. This was a blessing. Sunday morning had arrived, August 6, 2006. I must admit, the night before was restless. I tossed and turned all through the night. I sent up a strong prayer before I lay down, and all night long I was crying out to God in my sleeplessness. I needed the strengthening of worship service and fellowship, but was literally too weak and nervously sick to go to church. I simply had to get to a computer to review my grade. I waited until the library was opened, which seemed to take forever.

I was seated at the computer going through the motions of logging into the school's blackboard and it was as though I was looking through someone's eyes. And right before my eyes—or somebody else's—there, was my final grade. No suspense left—I didn't pass. I was lacking exactly seven points. Seven whole points! I did not fret. I could not fret. I just turned to my Heavenly Father in faith. I immediately connected with the spiritual significance of the number seven—the number of completion. I had a deep feeling in my soul that things were turning around. This was not evident based on what I could see with my natural eyes, but through the eyes of faith there was much evidence. You will see in a moment how I was blessed in all this. I now understand the depths of Hebrew 12:11, "Faith is the substance of things hoped for and the evidence of things not seen."

I needed only seven points, and it was proven that God was (and is) faithful. He proved that He would not leave or forsake me. The instructor had given us an optional project to do at the beginning of the course. Believe it or not, this project was worth—seven points. I said to myself, "Thank you God! I can handle this with your help!" Later, I called my instructor to inquire about the details of the project. I know he could feel the concern in my voice. He replied, "You can do the project, but it's less likely that students will receive the maximum amount of points." After his response, I briefly paused and asked God silently, "Where do I go from here?"

After a silent pause, he immediately shared that he would consider assigning another project, a report on Public Education Funding, but he would have to weigh it all out. A certain level of peace came over me instantly—that peace that is spoken about in (Philippians 4:7)—the peace that surpasses all understanding. I remember saying to myself, "Look at God work." All I needed was a little seed of hope. This hope was translated as the mercy, grace, and favor of God.

Phyllis, one of three prayer partners, truly a prayer warrior, prayed for hours, speaking life into this situation, praising God in advance for His seven-point miracle. She stated: "It's done." We were in total agreement. Vince and I prayed after this. His statement was, "Yo, you know God would not have brought you this far to leave you. You're at the end now, and I'll do all I can to help you."

After a few days had passed, I spoke with my instructor, and he explained that he had gone ahead to approve the second project because he felt strongly that the first project would prove far too challenging to receive the maximum points needed—for me, the seven points were absolutely necessary.

The enemy, the adversary, Satan, the devil himself—was mad. The furnace was turned up to a couple notches from the max. That is to say, those things were heating up on a level that only God could cool. Before things would cool down some, I received the second eviction notice. By now it was mid-August. I had only three days to move. Three days. I knew staying focused was not an option. God had proven He had not given up on me. I had to prove I would under no circumstances give up on God.

My plate was full. I was facing eviction with limited funds to move. I had a case study to do for the management class that normally required a group of two to three people. Then, there were two projects to finish for my financial analysis class. On top of all this, I was a single mother, with the sole responsibility to take care of my children. My heart was aching to spend more time with them—which had been limited due to the demands of school. Our transportation we could no longer call "ours," and as for our home, our apartment, it did not even feel the same. As I packed my things, my thoughts went from the journey in my life to this point. The bitter and sweet times in life make our life rich in so many ways. It might not always feel good or be consistent with the way we desire things to go, but God knows best. He was blessing me to learn. I was battling to earn my degree and yearning for a major change. My son, daughter, and I continued to pray. This is something we did no matter what. We have always prayed for others, even for the people who were speaking against us. This does happen, you know. But anyway, it was time to move.

On August 18, 2006, I moved in with one of my younger sisters. She kindly opened her door to the children and me. It was rather crowded and uncomfortable. The atmosphere was far different than what the three of us had grown to cherish in our former home. Yes, former. This was the new reality, so I just thanked God and reminded myself, "Not my will but God's will be done." Time was marching on. With no transportation, no computer, and with no help from the project partner and classmate I had worked with off and on all year, or any other classmate, three research projects were due. Once again, God had it worked out. Once again, my good friend was there.

Vince would take me to work and pick me up, until one of my coworkers moved in the same apartment complex that my sister was living in. She politely gave me a ride to work daily. He would then pick me up in the evenings. We would get to the library between 5:30 p.m. and 6:00 p.m., depending on his schedule and night of the week concerning library hours. Most nights we would be there until 9:00 p.m. when the library closed. I would get home sometimes around 10:00 p.m., sometimes later. I was away from home from 7:00 a.m. until whenever I got home routinely for more than a month. I was tired. Vince was worn out. But by the grace of God, we kept pressing on. And it was only because of His strength that we were able to press on.

Remember I shared Vince's response to these extra projects? I shared that he had told me that God had not brought me this far to leave me, and that he would do all he could to help. There was something always turning over in both our minds at the time—the vision that God had given Vince. Before he had met me, he knew me in a sense. God prepared him for the mental, emotional, and spiritual assignment in my life. It was revealed that we had blessed each other.

God had placed us in each other's life to help get each other to the next level. Vince had told me this from the very beginning. At the time in my brokenness I was thinking he could be my husband. He was different than any man I had met. I could tell that he felt the same although he expressed it as well. We connected on a spiritual level. We were both loving and caring and giving. We both loved God.

Yet, here was God loving both of us enough to refocus our attention whenever thoughts of being in a relationship came into play. It has not been easy, we certainly have had our confusing times, yet he and I was always reminded of what God spoke to him months before we came into each other's life—you'll be a blessing to one another. You will help each other get to the next level. Stay focused.

This brings me to this point. During this season in my life it was this focus that helped me make it through. I was definitely moving toward the next level. During this time in my "recovery" stage, God had been delivering me from relationship dependency and centering me upon the foundation of depending solely on Him. This brings me to the second point. Vince and I were purposed to be in each other's life. Vince has mentioned over and over, there is a difference between godly intent and what God, Himself, has intended. Sometimes we have sincere reasons or godly motives behind our thoughts, feelings, words, and actions—we must always be clear on whether or not this is what God has intended.

My final point is this. God knew that Vince had gone through enough storms to help me navigate my way through the storms. He sent a man to be a true friend to me. This is something I had never experienced. It was so hard at times for both of us. Yet, we kept our focus, and God truly blessed me with a friend to help me get to the next level. Not only was he there mentally, spiritually, emotionally, financially, but even socially.

Now, finally around the middle of September two out of three of the projects were submitted. It was during this time that God revealed my purpose. Actually, I was engaged in a conversation with Vince after he had picked me up from work. He mentioned how much of a blessing all of the stress and strain of school, coupled with other issues really were to both of us. He mentioned how much I had grown since we had met and especially in this season. He shared his thoughts about several of the experiences in meeting women that were at crossroads in their lives. Yes, I met so many women, young and old, that were so comfortable in opening up to share their stories or challenges with me. Vince remembered this and had recognized early in our friendship his belief that I was definitely purposed for ministry on a large scale. My first message at the church I delivered had been on guess what? Virtue.

We talked about the amazing journey, and there was a peace in me that was so different. As we talked, I relived the process of discovery that God had used with each and every one of these women—through me—my own experiences. I recalled the dream I had shared with Vince and a few others where I was standing on a platform ministering to thousands. Not long after my dream, Shundala, my high school classmate, friend, and co-worker on the job, told me about her having the identical vision. Not to mention, the countless times my former pastor shared this with me. It was clear.

My purpose was clear. I was to minister to women everywhere who were broken, many not knowing that they are broken or how they got there. I was to serve God as a vessel to help these women move from being victims of brokenness to virtuous and whole in the Heavenly Father. This is when Vince said, "I told you that what we often go through is for other people. Everything that God does is to strengthen us but it's never about us, it's about God, and He is about delivering His people from bondage. Yo, you've made it through, and you will go higher. You need to write a book."

I did not see quite this clearly during the storm. I do know this: no trial or tribulation is greater than God's purpose for our life. Oftentimes it is because of our purpose that we go through the trials and tribulations. There is nothing too hard for God. And God allowed me to connect my passion for wanting to be a blessing to women and my desire to want to bless women's lives with the many storms I had faced in my life, starting from childhood. Upon deciding to write this book my passion to help women increased tremendously and instantly.

I submitted my last school project around the middle October. By the end of October, I had received the final grades for all the subjects. Guess what? I did not *just* pass—I passed them all! I thanked God and gave Him all the glory! I will always remember how He placed a friend in my life that truly did stick closer than a brother—someone to help me weather the storms—someone fearless against the odds.

I was looking forward to December 14, 2006—my graduation day! When my name was called, I could hear my daughter screaming to the top of her lungs, "That's my mother!" I can never forget my son's big smile. I can remember the teary eyes of my friend, Vince. I will always remember his daughters' presence and laughter. And, oh, my friend Marisa—she made it possible for me to get to Montgomery, Alabama, that day. We all packed in her SUV and set out for Davis Theatre, where I walked across the stage to receive a reward for research, countless hours of studying, dedication, and perseverance. I give thanks to God, who is so awesome!

In all that happened during and before grad school, and no doubt after, God was preparing me for my special service to others. He was preparing me for ministry, in the true essence of the word ministry, which simply means "service." To live life based on serving others is a great place to be. It was Jesus who stated, "The greatest among you shall be your servant" (Matthew 23:11)

> *No matter what trial comes your way, continue to hold on to God's unchanging hand. There is no trial or tribulation greater than the power that God has bestowed upon you—you can make it through it, if you BELIEVE, PRAY, have FAITH, and take ACTION.*

THIS IS MY PRAYER TO OUR HEAVENLY FATHER FOR YOU AS YOU READ ON:

Father God, I have released this book in the hands of your daughters, now have your way. I pray that you will open up their ears so they will hear your word that has been expressed through a willing vessel which you have chosen. Help set them free from what they have so freely given themselves to. They have been confined. Many of them have been repeating so many negative life cycles, but through your healing and delivering power, I know they are free. I pray that they will come to know you, and will desire to have a relationship with you, Lord.

I pray that they will walk in virtue, and be the best examples of virtue before their daughters, sons, others, and most of all, to you. Some of them have been seeking you, but you seem to be so far out of reach and because of this, their faith has decreased. I pray that you will increase their faith. Father, their tears have filled their pillows; their friends are few; their families are judgmental; their co-workers are jealous; some of their church members are too religious; and they have felt no love at all! The counterfeited love that they have been feeling in the world cannot match your LOVE. They need you, God! Hold them. Comfort them. Guide them. I pray that you will show them your face as they read this book. Open up their spiritual eyes so that they can see the blessings you have set before them, and run the race of victory. Open up their spiritual ear gates so that they can hear your still small voice. Speak to their hearts, and transform their minds. Father God, teach them how to be sensitive to each other's needs, and bless them to make peace with all people. Teach them how to pray. Lord, increase their understanding, knowledge, and wisdom! I pray that they will listen, and heed your voice. You have made us to be nurturers, now help those who are struggling in that area. Help them to understand that we are your righteousness. Bless them to remain holy in their bodies and acceptable in your sight, for their body is the temple of you. I pray that they will walk in obedience, and they will become more vigilant. Purify their hearts, and most all bless all of us to walk in LOVE. I pray for your grace and mercy on us all. I bless your name. I honor you. I glorify you. I praise your name. You are truly worthy of all my praise. I give you the highest praise. Hallelujah! Hallelujah! I pray in your Son Jesus' name. Amen.

CHAPTER 1

A ROAD MAP TO VIRTUE... CRACKING THE SHELL TO BREAK THE YOLK

"The Lord is nigh unto them that are of a broken heart..."
(Psalm 34:18)

IF you had the money to travel to any destination you had in mind, where would it be? Well, some of us might say Bahamas, Jamaica, or Hawaii, just to name a few. Most of you do like to travel, right? Of course, in this instance, it may require air travel. Here is an illustration I would like to show you that requires a roadmap, which is used to help get us from one destination to the next. With this example, we will choose the same place to go—let us say, Rhode Island. Mind you, I am trying to go somewhere with this illustration.

Some of us will have shorter routes, and some will have longer routes. Since there are different routes, there will be people who will come to bumpy roads, dead end streets, have multiple hills to pull, and so on. But we will all get to our destination if the directions are followed as given on this roadmap. When we finally arrive at our destination, we will see how valuable this roadmap really is.

Some of us may turn around because the journey seems to long, and some may decide not to go at all. Now that is not to say that those who turn around and stop midways will not eventually get there. They might just need some encouragement along the way. Those who decide not to go will need an extra push.

The conclusion of this illustration is that God works just the same as a roadmap. He, in essence, is the roadmap. He wants to guide us from one destination to the next—take us from level to level—even higher than our minds can conceive. Many of us might get off course, lose focus, but we will all arrive there someday.

You see, we all started out when we were conceived in our mother's womb. We were all birthed with a purpose. We all have a destiny to fulfill. We all face difficult circumstances that life may present to us. More importantly, we were all born with the seed of virtue. We are all God's daughters, and He loves us so much, more than we will ever know.

There is something that I would like to share though—many of us are broken. To help you understand what I mean by broken, I will give you this analogy: If you were to pour water in a glass and it shatters as you pick it up off the table, then your water will spill, right? Once that glass shatters it can no longer be used for what it should be used for—and that is to drink liquid {water, juice soda} from. We as human are the same way—if we are shattered (broken) how can we be effective? I want you to understand that people can be broken in many areas of their lives. This would include mentally, emotionally, socially, or spiritually.

Therefore, we must use this roadmap (God) to guide us through these bumpy roads, take us around these dead end streets, and help us pull these hills of low self-esteem, bitterness, envy, jealousy, gossip; these things can delay us from getting to our destination. These are obstacles placed in our path by the enemy, who I will share more about later. In the meantime, let us use our roadmap (God) to get us to our destiny.

Here are some questions for you to consider:

- Are you broken?
- Do you know of someone who is mentally, emotionally, socially or spiritually broken?
- Are you striving to make sense out of the chaos and move toward becoming whole?
- Have you been praying and hoping for change?
- Have you been seeking professional, spiritual/pastoral counsel

or counsel from others?
- Have you found yourself repeating the same negative life cycles over and over again?
- Are you having a hard time letting go of your past hurt, pains, disappointments, and failures?
- Are you striving to become virtuous?

A VIRTUOUS WOMAN BUT BROKEN

Out of the millions upon millions of women in the world, there are a substantial number who are virtuous, but broken. The brokenness that you are experiencing could have possibly started in your childhood. So many women are having issues now, because of childhood scars. Whether it was your father, mother, brother, sister, extended relative, even a stranger who hurt or confused you—the adversity on your life has been crippling.

It is a blessing that you are now taking this very important step to overcome all the factors that have been hindering your growth and progress toward uncovering (discovering) just who God has purposed you to be. Who you are according to His will is more important and bigger than who caused your brokenness or in what ways you are broken, so go ahead, you can shout now. Your help is on the way. It is here, and it starts with you.

Once I admitted (confessed) that I was a broken vessel, I was able to take a step toward deliverance and freedom, yet this started with admitting the problem and being open and honest about the details surrounding the problem. With this openness God blessed me to uncover many of the actions and the words that were at the root of my dilemma. Discovering the causes of brokenness is essential after you have confessed. Once you admit brokenness, God, along with your new understanding and knowledge in the matter—a desire for change with a commitment to change—will now move you forward to a new you.

I now realize that you can be bound for so long, experiencing a life of unhappiness, still not able to identify that you are a broken vessel.

You know, I would probably describe brokenness as having a migraine headache. If you have ever experienced having a migraine headache, then you know exactly how it feels. Seemingly, all you desire to do as your head is pounding is take an aspirin or something to take the pain away. Ladies, we all desire that something to take the pain away.

Well, brokenness is like a spiritual migraine headache. Now just like you have a migraine headache, and you desire what's necessary to take the pain away, for those of you who have come to know that you are broken, whether it be spiritually, mentally, socially, or emotionally, you have recognized the signs and symptoms, and you have admitted it, now you have a desire to change so that you can move in the direction toward wholeness. You have noticed the negative life cycles you have repeated over and over again, due to your brokenness.

On the other hand, there are some of you who are broken, but do not know it. In essence, your brokenness is just like a silent migraine headache. You can feel the pain of a migraine headache, and you notice the signs and symptoms of it, unlike the silent migraine headache, the signs and symptoms are there, but you cannot feel the pain. Now just imagine not treating this pain, even though you cannot feel it. What do you think will happen? Now pain that is not properly treated can become more damaging—and it can affect so many other areas of the human body— it is like a silent killer. Again, you know the signs and symptoms are there, but there is still a tendency to desire that "something" to suppress what is not even felt. In the case of brokenness, seemingly you know you are repeating these negative life cycles, but because you do not know you are broken, you tend to treat this unfelt hurt and pain with more men, substances, or other so-called remedies. You see, being broken in one area can affect other areas of your life.

A woman who is broken on any level shows it on her face. No cosmetic can cover up her brokenness. It is also shown through your actions and conversation—all driven by your thoughts. Oftentimes those who were once broken, but are now whole and free from brokenness may notice that something is wrong. They can identify with the unfelt pain of that silent headache (brokenness) that you could not feel. You must realize through their deliverance, you can truly feel the confidence that you, too, can be delivered.

It was a blessing when that ministering angel came into my life and helped me to identify with my brokenness. I did not fully understand the dynamics of my brokenness and how it played a major part in my doing things contrary to God's will, but I am grateful that it was revealed to me. I thank Him for freedom. I decree that you too will find freedom and be released from the shackles of brokenness—this is your season.

PRAYER:
Lord, I confess that I am broken, but I know that I am healed, delivered, and set free through your great healing powers. I know that I am made whole. I know that I can do all things through you who strengthens me. I thank you for giving me that faith to move this mountain.

AFFIRMATION:
I will focus on moving in the direction of healing daily. I will see myself whole, happy, and confident.

UNCOVERING THE SEEDS OF BROKENESS

We often wonder why so many women are broken, but most broken women have a hard time facing the root causes of brokenness. Your mother, grandmother, and great-grandmother may have been broken. The moment our mothers were conceived in brokenness, we were being shaped in it, which could very well be identified as a generational curse. We oftentimes limit generational curses to adultery, lying, drunkenness, and many other obvious sins, but brokenness can lead to many other sins mentioned in the Bible that are contrary to God's will. Do you remember me mentioning the woman at the well? Well, if you have read this story you will find that this woman had been with several men—and none of them was her husband. Jesus knew it. She knew it. But because of her brokenness, she had opened herself up to these adulterous relationships or possibly even multiple marriages.

A lot of you may have witnessed some sort of abuse in the home when you were little innocent children. You did not know why things happen the way they did, but nonetheless—it did. Behind witnessing such horrible acts, some of you have been left scarred, but I am convinced through my healing, you can also experience healing and deliverance through the transformation of your minds. In Proverbs 23:7 we read, "...For as he thinketh in his heart, so is he..." You should begin speaking life into your situation. If you think that you can be healed, then that is where your mind and heart will take you, toward healing. On the other hand, if you are thinking and speaking on bad things—there it is, you have just given the enemy legal right to come in and do whatever he pleases. Your thoughts of freedom can lead to freedom.

TRUE STORY

I know of a lady who had been abused from conception to adulthood. One day she felt the need to share her story. I can tell that she had been holding a lot on the inside that was ready to be openly expressed. I told her that she can find freedom, healing, and deliverance by admitting and confessing what has been causing her pain and hurt for more than 50 years.

She emphatically expressed how her father treated her so differently from her sisters. He was very mean, she said. He would buy her sisters clothes, shoes, and other things, without buying her anything. You know those kinds of things every child desires. Any tangible items she received came from her mother. "Why?" I asked. "I don't know why, but it was very hurtful to me," she said.

She went on to say that her mother had given her permission to go to a birthday party one night, and when she arrived home from the party her father had an extension cord ready to whip her. She ran up the street—over an older lady's house in the neighborhood—for safety. I asked, "Why did he want to whip you?" And she replied, "I don't know. My mother had given me permission to go to the party."

Later, at the age of 16, she graduated from high school. Strangely, when she arrived home on the night of her graduation, he viciously told her to leave his house. While she was excited and expecting to receive a reward for her accomplishment, like most high school graduates, he could only reward her with a gift of confusion and anger. This was a sad graduation gift, right? I was teary-eyed after hearing this.

After having to leave with nowhere to go, she was compelled to gain the help of this man who was a father figure in her life, yet he was a man whose eyes fell upon her at the age of fifteen. Oh, my God! She told him that her father put her out so she did not have anywhere to go. Yes, he offered her assistance by opening up his doors, but shacking up, or living with a man without being married to him, was not an option, she said. She told him she could not live with him unless he married her.

Now it was five months after graduation, she had turned 17 years old and was made his wife. I asked, "Why did you marry this man who was old enough to be your father?" and "Did you think about what you were doing?" "No," She replied. "I really didn't think about it until after I married him."

Later, she gave birth to her firstborn at the age of 18—more children came later—more than she had planned to have. I asked, "Why did you have more than you desired?" and "Did you want to go to college?" Well, "He wanted more children," And, "Yes, I went to three different colleges, but I didn't finish."

Well, here is what was shocking—when she turned 30 years old; she learned that the man she thought was her father was not! Wow! This was interesting. One day, they had a heated argument and he yelled, "You're not my (blank) daughter anyway." He said it out of anger and bitterness, she said. This was the only man she had known from birth up to the point she was put out of his house—he was her daddy.

A few days later, an older lady down the street invited her into her home to show her a picture of her biological father. She was stunned, after seeing the picture of her stepfather and biological father taken together. They both went to the same church—and served as deacons. Sadly, she never had the opportunity to meet her biological father. By the time she learned of him, he had died. She was told that she had other sisters. As she reflected upon her childhood, she remembered the girls she went to the party with the night her mom gave her permission—those were her other sisters! She had seen them several times but never knew them beyond the neighborhood.

Now this lady's rights of knowing her father were taken away as a child. Her mother never told her because of the shame and guilt she faced as a result of going outside of her marriage to conceive a child—who was innocent all along—by someone who went to the same church their family were members of. After learning about her biological father, she asked her mother, but the truth was never offered. Her mother began to distance herself, only to hold the golden key to every child's right (isolation is not good when it comes to something of this magnitude; your child should know the truth). In her innocence, she was mentally, emotionally, socially, and physically abused by a man who never received her and a mother who held back the truth that was worth her knowing. Where do you think all this madness can lead to?

You see, she was conceived in adultery, never felt loved by her stepfather, never knew her biological father, never had a healthy childhood, forced to transition from a child to a wife within six months, and accept the abuse from a man who was more than twenty years senior to her. This was compounded abuse because it started with the man who raised her. This, in and of itself, is a lot to carry for year after year. She was broken, now fighting to find freedom.

In this instance, this lady was able to reflect upon her childhood to gain a clearer understanding of why she had been bound for so long. She was determined to uncover the seeds of brokenness and release the pains and hurts of her past, yet she did not admit (or truly not aware) that she was broken so that she could take the necessary steps toward freedom.

PRAYER:
Lord, I thank you for giving me the wisdom and understanding of where my brokenness came from. I thank you that I am no longer hidden in the shadow of brokenness. I thank you for giving me the power to break this cycle of brokenness.

AFFIRMATION:
I choose to live mentally, spiritually, and physically and not die mentally, spiritually, and physically. I declare the works of the Lord.

THE AFFECTS OF BROKENESS AND VIRTUE

Brokenness can have so many barriers on virtue. Some of these barriers could be bitterness, unhappiness, anger, being unforgiving, not knowing how to communicate in a calm manner, and so forth. These barriers can hinder us from being all we need to be in our family, and even our friends' lives.

Being broken has also caused many of us to even make the same high impact decisions repeatedly—namely bad relationship choices—that are dysfunctional. Some of us may or may not realize when we choose to invite a certain type of man in our life, whether he's good or bad, broken or whole, it is a strong reflection of who we are. Granted, we all make frivolous decisions sometimes.

I can remember the time I was broken and how it affected me personally. Because of my brokenness, I started to isolate myself, which made it very difficult for me to receive my healing and walk in wholeness. I was not being open and honest with myself. The isolation did not make my situation better. I was in denial.

Strangely, God sent a ministering angel after I admitted that I had a problem and recognized the reality of being caught up in these negative cycles, which produced the same negative results. My friend, Vince, saw that I was a broken vessel. He encouraged me to move forward because there is so much more to life than being trapped in the prison of brokenness.

I have now learned that we must be open to share with others so that we can propel toward our destiny—with no negatives affecting us, our virtue—due to brokenness.

PRAYER:
Lord, I thank you now for healing and teaching me how to deal with my brokenness.

AFFIRMATION:
Brokenness will no longer have an adverse affect on my life. From this day forward, I choose to be happy and strive for perfection. I will wake up happy and go to bed happy, knowing I am who God says I am, and I am healed from this brokenness.

THE IMPORTANCE OF VISUALIZING WHO YOU ARE

It is important that you answer the following questions so that you can visualize who you are. The answers to these questions determine whether or not you see yourself in a negative or positive way.

- Can you see the true image of yourself?
- Do you see yourself in a negative image?
- Do you see yourself in a positive image?
- Do you see yourself as being an unattractive woman?
- Do you see yourself as being an attractive woman?
- Do you see yourself as a progressive woman?
- Do you see yourself as an unsuccessful woman?
- What conclusion can you draw from this?
- Is it possible you may have low self-esteem?
- If so, where does that come from?
- Did something happen to you in your childhood or adulthood?
- Were you talked about all the time as a child?
- Were you called ugly?
- Were you called fat?

- Were you told that you would not make it far in life?
- Were you molested?
- Did all this leave you broken?

You must know that you are truly the righteousness of God. You are beautiful and smart—full of talent and gifts, no matter who says you are not. There was something significant about all of us from the moment God put Adam to sleep and took one of his ribs. He saw fit to create us from the supernatural work of His spiritual hands. He shaped and formed us perfectly. In His creating us, He knew exactly what He was doing. That means you are definitely not a mistake. We possess so much, but because of the lies the devil has told us, many women struggle with the acceptance of who they are.

Once the negative images of yourself have been planted in your mind, the tendency to attract negative things in your life will be great—the law of attraction is now in full effect. Your drive to move forward is not even there after the negative images have been planted. If you think about all the negative things that have been said or have happened to you from childhood up to this point, I am certain it has hindered you in ways you could not believe. For example, if someone told you that you are not beautiful enough to become a model, and you have been called ugly all your life, then this seed will be planted. You have now accepted that in your spirit because you do not feel that your nose is perfectly shaped, or your lips are not right, or you do not have the right texture of hair. Your hopes and dreams of becoming a model have now faded. Another example is if someone told you that you are not smart enough to obtain a degree. You accept the fact that you had certain learning issues as a child, and now you do not feel that you are capable of learning college coursework, so you never go. Lastly, someone told you that you cannot sing. You begin to think about all of those times you could not stay in tune, so you have given up. Do you see how negative thoughts can produce negative images, which, in turn, lead to negative outcomes?

It is necessary to change the way you visualize yourself. If you will notice, actions are driven by visualization, and visualization is driven by thoughts. You see, to start you will **think** about the negative or positive, then you begin to **see** whatever that something is, then you paint a mental picture, if you will, and then you **act**. Did you get that? Here are the ingredients. **Think. Visualize. Act.** Whether it is negative or positive, that is totally up to you. Just for a moment, I want you to think about all the negative things someone told you, whether it was your mother, father, sister, brother, friend, or anyone else for that matter. Now just as you painted a mental picture of all those negative things, and found yourself acting on it, I want you to replace all those negative things with positive thoughts. Do this in your mind now. You know what those things are, so go ahead, and picture them in a positive image. Can you see? What does it look like?

Is it the woman who was called ugly as a little girl who always dreamed of becoming a model, and now she is walking down the runway? Is it the woman who had those learning challenges as a little girl who always wanted to obtain a degree, and now receiving a diploma in her hand? Is it the woman who struggled with staying in tune as a little girl singing in the choir who always dreamed of becoming the "next American Idol," and now she has a record deal?

I was a woman who did not feel beautiful on the outside because my self-esteem had been attacked as a child. I was completely broken. I bore the hurt of what I was told as a child, and even what happened to me as a child. I carried that through my teens and into my early adulthood, but when I was made whole—totally delivered from people—I learned to accept everything about me. Outer beauty with respect to trying to please people can be an enemy of your destiny. It is never the outer appearance that matters; it is what is on the inside of you that will take you to greater heights and fulfill your ultimate destiny.

Once you are healed on the inside, you can better serve God and the manifestation of His glory will draw people to a wonderful, beautiful, anointed, spirit-filled woman. When you realize that you are only a tool used by God, you begin to care less of what people think and say about you and more of who He has made and declared you to be. To add to this, begin to replace all the negative images with positive ones.

When you do that, you will see a major difference in your life.

> *PRAYER:*
> *I am the righteousness of you, Lord. You are worthy of all my praise. There is nothing that can separate me from your unconditional love and kindness. I thank you that my inner beauty reflects my outer beauty. Lord, I know that I do not need any man to validate me—for I am a woman of God—filled with your holy spirit, but help me to accept and appreciate how you created me.*

> *AFFIRMATION:*
> *I will continue to tell myself that I am the righteousness of God. I was beautiful as a child. I am beautiful now, and forever will be. And I have a beautiful heart, and this I know. "I can do all things through Christ who strengthens me" (Philippians 4:13).*

NURTURING SELF DURING DELIVERANCE

Thank the Lord that you are on a path of deliverance. Do not think that you are by yourself. You just continue walking in your season of deliverance. God has people who are willing to help you while you are on your journey. While you are in this season of deliverance, pamper yourself from time to time—go shopping, to the salon, movies. You can even participate in church activities, including women's retreats so that you can be around other women who are on the road to deliverance and virtue. You can even find time to read uplifting, inspirational books by others who share their stories of healing and deliverance.

Jesus came to heal the broken-hearted and set the captives free, but He needs your help—give your life to Him—submit now.

> *PRAYER:*
> *Lord, I thank you for delivering me from every trial and tribula-*

tion. I can shout Glory, even now.

AFFIRMATION:
From now on, I will see myself as overcoming all my obstacles; delivered, and set free no matter what trials come my way.

HOW TO HELP IDENTIFY BROKENNESS IN YOURSELF AND OTHERS

There are many ways to identify brokenness in yourself and others. The first step is self-examination. This requires uncovering these issues through observation, contemplation, meditation, communication with self, and most of all, prayer. There will be some of you who will be cognizant of certain patterns in your lives. With this being said, it is easier for you to detect that there is a magnetic force—a certain "vibration" within your soul that causes you to attract adverse circumstances, all surrounding your brokenness. This can be avoided, once you become more vigilant, if you will. Have you found yourself leaving one relationship and moving in the direction of another before you have had time to yourself? Have you noticed that you have been attracting the same type of men over and over again? These are the type of cycles you must look for in your life and others.

When you come to realize that you were once broken, and now made whole, you can recognize the brokenness of other women. You can detect the signs and symptoms of her brokenness—certain patterns in her life and more.

Some women have accepted the unacceptable because they have not accepted who they really are. They have no self-love, nor have they gained self-identity. Because of brokenness, we find ourselves opening up certain doors in our lives which seemingly take us backwards. We need to ask ourselves: How can I help a broken woman, if I am broken? The answer is: we can't.

PRAYER:
Lord, I thank you for healing me first so that I can help my sisters in Christ. I thank you for blessing me to share with my sisters all about your goodness and how you are always using willing vessels to help someone who needs healing.

AFFIRMATION:
I will encourage my sisters daily to be strong as I continue striving to be an example and reflection of my sisters' new-found freedom, strength, and identity in Christ.

A VIRTUOUS WOMAN BUT WHOLE

Oh, what a blessing it is to be a whole woman! This, in and of itself, can increase your spiritual growth and allow you to be all that God has purposed you to be. When you're whole, you can also help bring deliverance in the lives of others. Wholeness ultimately brings about freedom, which enables you to think outside the box. You will begin to think for yourself and not let others control you with their thinking. You will realize the importance of only God controlling your life, not a man, substances, or anything else.

There is a certain level of peace that comes with wholeness. You know, when you are peaceful, it releases positive energy in the atmosphere—in the home, at church, on the job—wherever you go. More importantly, wholeness will shed light on that seed of virtue (you) and make it flourish. I believe when you are whole, you can walk in your destiny. There is a strong tendency to stay focused when you are whole.

PRAYER 1:
Lord, I thank you for your love, grace, and mercy that sustain me through the years of pain! Thank you for giving me the courage, strength, and faith to face this pain and conquer all issues that have held me back from being the virtuous woman you purposed me to be.

PRAYER 2:
Lord, I thank you for making me whole. It is because of you that I can breathe, walk, talk, see, hear, feel and smell. I thank you Lord that I'm able to operate at full capacity. I thank you for blessing me to be the virtuous woman you have called me to be in my home, on my job, in the church, in the community. I am the light on the hill that cannot be hidden. Women from near and far are drawn to me because it is You who has exalted me. I can say from now on that "You are my shepherd: I shall not want. You maketh me to lie down in green pastures: You leadeth me beside the still waters. You restored my soul: You leadeth me in the paths of righteousness for Your name's sake...my cup runneth over; {I know I'm not deserving of all your goodness} but I thank you for Surely, Goodness and Mercy following me all the days of my life..." (Psalm 23)

AFFIRMATION:
I demand of myself; my thoughts, actions, and behavior that will be consistent with this new person you purpose me to be and I desire to become. I decree that I am made whole. I am healed mentally, physically, spiritually, socially, emotionally, and financially. I will never let a part of me be broken again. I will continue to tell myself that I am a virtuous woman. I will continue to tell myself that I am the righteousness of God. I will continue to tell myself that I will overcome all obstacles. I will continue to tell myself that I can do all things through Christ who strengthens me. I will continue to tell myself that I will be successful. I will continue to tell myself that I am beautiful, smart, intelligent, and anointed. I will continue to walk by faith and not by sight. I will continue to encourage other women. I will continue to speak those things that are not, as though they were. I will not let negativity dominate my thoughts. I will surround myself with positive people. I am confident in myself. I choose to be happy for the rest of my life.

CHAPTER 2

AMOROUS

"For God so loved the world that he gave his only begotten Son, that whosoever believeth in him should not perish, but have everlasting life."

(John 3:16)

I can remember when I was impatiently searching for love from men, leading to bad relationship choices. This was prior to recognizing that there are many types of love—the puppy love that later transitions into passionate love cannot match the love that God first showed us through His Son Jesus, which is called agape love. This is the type of love I have come to appreciate more than ever, and you should too.

LOVING UNCONDITIONALLY

It is time for us to stop putting conditions on our love for each other. God's love, agape love, is unconditional. It is not proud nor is it unruly. It does not have any stipulations or limits on how much He loves us. Also, God commanded that we love each other. It is the greatest commandment that He gave to us. Unconditional love is not like a faucet. You cannot just turn your love on and off. It is solid, real, longsuffering, patient and compassionate. There is no charge for you to love each other. And it should always be reciprocated, no matter what.

And you know what? You have to love your enemies! Yes, even the people who have despitefully used you, mistreated you, said bad things about you, and looked down on you. And this is when you have to love them more. Matthew 5:44 we read, "Love your enemies..."

1 Corinthians 13:1-13 says, *"Though I speak with the tongues of*

men and of angels and have not charity, I am become as sounding brass, or a tinkling cymbal. And though I have the gift of prophecy, and understand all mysteries, and all knowledge; and though I have all faith, so that I could remove mountains, and have no charity, I am nothing. And though I bestow all my goods to feed the poor, and though I give my body to be burned, and have not charity, it profiteth me nothing. Charity, suffereth long, and is kind; charity envieth not; charity vaunteth not itself, is not puffed up. Doth not behave itself unseemly, seeketh not her own, it is not easily provoked, thinketh no evil. Rejoiceth not in iniquity, but rejoiceth in the truth. Bereath all things, believeth all things, hopeth all things, edureth all things. Charity never faileth: but whether there be prophecies, they shall fail whether there be tongues, they shall cease; whether there be knowledge, it shall vanish away. For we know in part, and we prophesy in part, But when that which is perfect is come, then that which is in part shall be done away. When I was a child, I spake as a child, I understood as a child, I thought as a child, but when I became a man, I put away childish things. For now we see through a glass, darkly; but then face-to-face: now I know in part; but then shall I know even as also I am known. And now abideth faith, hope, charity, these three; but the greatest of these is charity."

As you can see, the Scripture shares with us the importance of charity, which is love. It does not matter what spiritual gifts you possess, if you do not have charity, you are not following God's word. This is not limited to spiritual gifts or worldly gifts, talents, college degrees or job status. I often reflect on how Jesus' ministry was and the true essence of His character while He was here. And one of His profound attributes that I find most admirable was His benevolence. He truly represented what real **LOVE** is and how it should be carried out throughout the world. And **LOVE** is not a matter of religion.

PRAYER:
Lord, I thank you for showing me your love and giving me the heart to love unconditionally.

AFFIRMATION:
I will love unconditionally daily.

WALK IN LOVE

Jesus walked the earth every day in love. Can you still walk in love when someone has violated you? Can you still walk in love when the money is low? Can you still walk in love when you have been rejected? Can you still walk in love when you do not hear it often—from your friend, mother, father, sister, brother, husband, or children? Can you still walk in love if your husband walked out on you? It does not matter who has offended you—you should still walk in love.

I can remember the times I was going through trials and tribulations. Although I did not feel the love of many who surrounded me, I still had to walk in love. I think sometimes your love is challenged. The enemy will bring circumstances to stand in the way of your walking in love like God encourages us to do in Scripture. This is to be applied to our daily lives. Do not let situations prevent you from loving each other, even when you do not feel it!

PRAYER:
Lord, I thank you for teaching me how to walk in love no matter what comes my way. I thank you for ordering my steps daily.

AFFIRMATION:
I will walk in love every day and make peace with all people.

SPEAKING LOVE

It is truly a blessing to feel the love behind words that are spoken so kindly by one who encourages, understands, and motivates you to press your way through the circumstances of life. Many have spoken words of encouragement in my life. I was able to connect with the love behind the words that were spoken. I expect to hear kind words daily, and you should too. I know that you can feel when someone speaks to you out of love. Everything should be done in love.

As I reflect on the negative and positive words spoken to me during the process of writing this book up to its completion, along with the rejection of the support of bringing this book to fruition, I still had to remain positive and keep my eyes on the vision so that I could walk in my destiny. And I had to continue to speak kind words during and after the rejection.

Here is an example of the impact kind words spoken in love can have in our lives. Just imagine arguing with someone who is very angry, or observe those who are in a heated argument. If you will pay close attention, you will notice that if both are calm and offering respect despite their difficulties, they are both able to resolve this issue, leaving each other's self-esteem and peace intact. They respect one another's point of view. Their objective is not to win the battle of who is right and who is wrong. They are simply trying to move toward understanding.

On the other hand, if you have one person calm and the other hostile, the hostile person is in an attack mode. Their sole objective is to be heard—to be understood—to be right. In this case, their adrenaline is very high and things are often stated by the hostile person that is very hurtful. However, the calmness of the other person has a way of causing the hostile person to calm down after a while. After the argument, there is often deep regret of the hostile person's behavior and a deep sorrow that forces an apology.

Now we all know that there are those who will not apologize no matter what. For those of us who never apologize, we have to bear the weight of stubbornness, sometimes for years. An apology does not mean we are wrong about the point we were trying to make during the argument—we simply apologize for behavior. We should do the same for others who argue in the spirit of anger. It does not mean they are right; it is just that holding grudges or resentment is out of character for those who "love."

We must forgive others in order for our Heavenly Father to forgive us. In Matthew 12:37 we read, "For by thy words thou shalt be justified, and by they words thou shalt be condemned." We are responsible for what we say. Furthermore, life and death is in the power of the tongue—it is during arguments, that anger and the need to be right cause us to speak negative words to the mind and heart of another person. In James 3:11 we read, "Doth a fountain send forth at the same place sweet water and bitter?"

No matter what, the person who is calm has a way that is truly pleasing in the sight of God, whether they are right or wrong. More importantly, when we calm down and stop defending our positions, we will find that the thoughts of others also have merit. We will often find that both are right, simply with a need to approach this matter in peace and love to gain understanding.

PRAYER:
Lord, I thank you for teaching me how to speak kind words of love from my heart. I thank you for blessing me not to defend my position, offending others by speaking negative words toward them.

AFFIRMATION:
I will speak words of life, love, joy, peace, and happiness each day. I will ask Him from this day forward to order my footsteps, and let the words flow from my mouth like a fountain that they will only be words that will produce good fruit—life.

GREETING WITH LOVE

How does it feel when someone walks up to you and embraces you with a hug that is full of love? Sometimes people just need a hug. You really never know how something as small as a hug can change a person's day. Just the compassion and love behind a hug can make a big difference in a person's life. You should always ask God on a daily basis, "How can I be a blessing to someone this day?" He will direct your every move.

The pastor at my former church always told us to greet each other every Sunday, before each worship service. We would walk around the church greeting each other with a big hug. Oh, I could just see how that hug would brighten the day of each church member. "It is a blessing to be a blessing," even with something as simple as a hug.

PRAYER:
Lord, I thank you that I can embrace someone with a hug. I thank you that I have the arms to wrap around someone to show them that unconditional love that you have bestowed upon me.

AFFIRMATION:
I will make a commitment to hug at least one person a day.

LOVE COVERS A FAULT

Do not become that person who loves to find fault in another person. We all have faults. None of us are so holy that we have never done anything wrong. You should walk in love and not point out a person's fault. In other words, do not be a faultfinder. If you think about it, the very fault you are pointing out in another person is one that you have or have been delivered from it. Instead of being a faultfinder, just substitute that with being a prayer warrior. Pray for your brother or sister.

Do not let a fault stand in the way of helping others. Jesus walked in love and He forgives us of our faults and shortcomings. When Jesus walked the earth healing, He did not ask the people of their faults. His love for them and their faith is what made them whole. He would tell them to go and sin no more. You should be more loving and forgiving too. In 1 Peter 4:8 we read, "And above all things have fervent charity among yourselves: for charity shall cover the multitude of sins (faults)."

PRAYER:
Lord, I thank you for covering my faults. I thank you for loving me enough to forgive me and still see me as your own.

AFFIRMATION:
I will self-examine myself daily and not point out the faults of

other people. I will continue to walk in love and forgiveness.

CHAPTER 3

VIGILANT

"Be sober; be vigilant; because your adversary the devil, as a roaring lion, walketh about seeking whom he may devour."

(1 Peter 5:8)

BEING vigilant is essential in our everyday life. When we lack vigilance, we tend to make poor decisions, and because of our choices, we can be drawn to do things that are totally contrary to the will of our Father. That common enemy is always planning and plotting to attack us through anything or anyone.

WHY IS IT SO IMPORTANT TO BE A SOBER-MINDED WOMAN?

Many of us do not think soberly. God has given some of us wisdom, but we do not to think rationally or objectively because of past pains/experiences, multiple addictions, and substance abuse—alcohol, drugs—or any number of other issues. Those dilemmas can cause us to remain stagnant, or not to grow, or to operate with the wisdom God has given us.

This is reflected in our personalities, which is often influenced by our mentalities. Our personalities are often shaped around our brokenness. It is this brokenness oftentimes, which creates a mindset, mentality that forces us in the opposite direction of truth, freedom, and peace.

I cannot stress this point enough. Some of the same bad mistakes we have repeatedly made or have been made are a result of our own thinking. Have you ever heard the saying, "A mind is a terrible thing to waste?" Well, many women can find themselves caught in the negative emotions of the moment. These negative emotions are what drive our thoughts, and this thinking is what causes us to make bad decisions.

These poor decisions also reflect our lack of vigilance. That means being watchful. We must observe what others say to us. More importantly, we must observe what we say to ourselves in the silence of our thoughts. It is our thoughts that provoke these negative emotions and thinking; and our thoughts that make us have spur-of-the moment choices—only to reap a negative outcome.

One of the symptoms of a bad mindset is how we negatively approach, respond, and behave in situations. This is possible because we always move in a direction of what we think about most, whether, regardless of whether that direction is negative or positive. But in this case, we are talking about wasting our thoughts, our time, and our energy in a way that is contrary to producing good fruit, or to producing a positive outcome. In essence, if we waste our time on negative issues, we are wasting our minds.

Now that you have identified the impact of a negative mindset, you know what is needed to challenge, correct, and move you toward a positive mindset. That movement should direct you toward success and freedom. When you think in the right direction, you can attract the right things in your life. Positive thoughts will attract positive results to result in your favor.

PRAYER:
Lord, I thank you for allowing me to keep a sober mind so that I can be open to truth and the direction that you are leading me. I thank you for helping me to think objectively and not subjectively.

AFFIRMATION:
I will think with an open mind daily, making wise decisions for my family and me, and think in the direction of great success. I will be open to expand my mind beyond religion and accept where God is leading me.

WATCH AS WELL AS PRAY

Matthew 26:41 says, "Watch and pray that ye enter not into temptation: the Spirit indeed is willing, but the flesh is weak."

Are you cognizant of your surroundings? Do you have a habit of only watching the small things in life? Does everything appear to be negative in your sight? Do not become that woman who falls for anything. Do not accept less than what God has intended for your life. When you begin to watch more, you will find that everything you have been looking for was there all along.

Do you pray often? Have you been asking God to show you something lately? Are you seeking answers? Remember, when you pray for something, you should expect to receive an answer from God. We tend to ask God for clarification or answers, but when He shows us, we are non-receptive or not willing to take heed. In James 5:16 we read, "...The effectual fervent prayers of a righteous man availeth much."

Jesus told His disciples to watch as He went to pray. When He returned He discovered that they all had fallen asleep. Matthew 26:38-40 says, "...My soul is exceeding sorrowful, even unto death: tarry ye here, and watch with me. And he went a little farther, and fell on his face, and prayed, saying, O my Father, if it be possible, let this cup pass from me: nevertheless not as I will, but as thou wilt. And he cometh unto the disciples, and findeth them asleep, and saith unto Peter. What, could ye not watch with me one hour?

I want you to think about a time you prayed for verification of the truth or instructions for your life—whether it was a confirmation of a man being your husband or if you should have relocated or if you should have accepted a particular job. Whatever it was that you were praying for, you were expecting an answer from God. Well, He showed you and gave you a clear vision and "Word," but you could not see it. Do you remember how it affected you? I am certain that whatever it is that you wanted, it was not good after all. Make no mistake about it. When God shows you something, and He answers your prayers, you need to take heed. Be very observant as you pray. Do not miss the mark because the prize does not always appear the way you expect it.

PRAYER:
Lord, I thank you for blessing me to be watchful as I pray for answers, instructions, and guidance for my life...

AFFIRMATION:
I decree to watch as much as I pray. I will take heed to the revelations that are revealed to me, and the instructions that are given to me.

WATCHING WITH YOUR SPIRITUAL EYES

It is a blessing for you to see with your natural eyes. It is truly a blessing and a gift from God to behold His glory in a sunset, to watch your children grow up. It is a blessing to be able to identify the many signs given in observing someone close to you, which indicates their joys and pain, and/or the role we must play in offering our help. In addition, He has given us spiritual eyes to capture what happens in the spiritual realm—discernment—another gift.

God has allowed women to have what we call, a woman's intuition. When I think of intuition, it is no more than a spirit of discernment. I am certain many of you have said to yourselves, "I should have gone with my first mind," "I knew something wasn't right about that," or "My intuition told me something was wrong." You have probably used one of those statements at least once, and in most cases, you were right.

Discernment, or spiritual intuition, is a gift from our Heavenly Father and it allows us to see, hear, and feel the truth of matters regardless of what seems to be happening on a physical level. Being vigilant makes you heed to that voice that softly speaks to your spirit telling you to pray/intercede for someone who may be having certain challenges in their life. There are times that voice might say, *"Do not go that way!"* For instance, you might have been on your way to work, taking one route, and you heard that still small voice. Later, you found out that God was taking you around an accident. You thanked Him for His direction because you realized it could have been you who were involved in that accident. What about the time that voice said, "Call *a certain friend you have not seen in a while,*" or *"Do not mess with that man; he is no good for you*! "There is so much more we can discern on a spiritual level.

Living in a world of confusion, contradictions, selfishness, even wickedness and malice, you must be able to be vigilant because we all share a common enemy. This enemy can come in the form of family members, friends, co-workers—anyone can be used by this enemy to cause us to act in ways that are contrary to God's will. This enemy always seeks to thwart the manifold blessings of truth, love, happiness, peace, joy, wisdom, knowledge, understanding—key ingredients to your growth and virtue." (1 Peter 5:8).

> *PRAYER:*
> *Lord, I thank you for giving me eyes to see all of the natural things that you have formed for mankind. I thank you for allowing me to see with the spiritual eyes that you have given me. The dreams and visions that you have allowed me to see have been an awesome experience. The discernment that you have given to me has allowed me to turn from what I am drawn to with my natural eyes. Lord, help me to walk in it every day.*

> *AFFIRMATION:*
> *I will open up my spiritual eyes to see my daily surroundings, and take heed to your truth.*

CAN YOU SEE SPIRITUALLY WHO YOU ARE IN A RELATIONSHIP WITH AND/OR MARRIED TO?

Many of you have been in relationships/marriages for 10, 30, or even 50 years, but you have not been with the man God has purposed for you. My friend, Vince, would say many times that a lot of women are with "*a* man," not "*the* man." I can remember praying before I entered each relationship, that the man I was involved with would be "*the* man" God had for me. Strangely, none of them were. Obviously, I was not the one for them either. You see, I have learned that there is a difference. A man is just what he is—"*a* man." He can be a pastor, bartender, salesman, truck driver, foreman, engineer, broker, chief executive officer, entrepreneur, painter, actor—it does not even matter. These are titles that separate them.

Just because he is "*a* man" does not mean he is "*the* man" God has purposed for you. Ladies, it starts with you meeting "*a* man." He looks good. He has a beautiful home. He has a lot of money. He has a nice car. He has a good job. In sum, this is "*a* man" that's got it going on. What attracted you? Mind you, "*a* man" can have all the good qualities you have desired—he buys you the fancy roses, diamond rings, he tells you he loves you, respects and honors you, opens the door for you, treats your children with kindness, wines and dines you—oh, he even goes to church. I mean, he is the one you have always dreamed of.

Listen, this is not a judgment call. Some of you are married to pastors, and other men who hold big titles. Maybe I am stepping on some toes at this point. You see, pastors can be just "*a* man," and not "*the* man." You may have been drawn to him because he is truly anointed—knowledgeable with great understanding, high level of wisdom, operating with many spiritual gifts. In all of his spiritual assets, he can have material ones that will catch the attention of the most financially well-to-do women or a woman struggling financially. However, none of this means that he is "*the* man" for you.

There are many women who find themselves caught up in the prestige of being the wife or significant of those wearing titles, whether the obsession is being the pastor's wife, or the first lady of the church, or even saying, "Dr. so and so's wife." Not to mention, the other vast number of men we often seek such as a professional athlete, "*a* man" or those in the entertainment field, a business or anyone we feel will satisfy us emotionally by giving us bragging rights or our need to be esteemed by others.

There are times "*a* man" can come into your life to truly be a blessing on some level, but there are other times "*a* man" can come into your life to cause harm. This does not have anything to do with his title either—he can even be the pastor. Let me ask again: "What attracted you to this man?"

You see, "*a* man" can criticize you, cheat on you, disrespect you, not love you, or outright mistreat you—but that depends on his character, not his title. A title does not separate the characteristics of a man, or anyone for that matter. When you open yourself up to this type of man, you may experience unhappiness, frustration, confusion, and manipulation all over again. Once you start a relationship with this man, later you find yourself in a trap. Just like a spider's web (you know it is there), but when you try to eradicate it, you cannot always remove it because the web is now what I call a "web of emotions."

Your emotions can sometimes be good or bad, unhealthy or healthy, yet the "web of emotions" we are now addressing is bad and unhealthy. Many of you have let your emotions lead you into these harmful relationships because you were not watching with your spiritual eyes, some have even identified real love with the materials "*a* man" give them. What are your values as a woman? What kind of standards have you set? Are they godly or ungodly? Please read:

Roman 8:5-9, "For they that are after the flesh do mind the things of the flesh; but they that are after the Spirit the things of the Spirit. For to be carnally minded is death, but to be spiritually minded is life and peace. Because the carnal mind is enmity against God: for it is not subject to the law of God, neither indeed can be. So then they that are in the flesh cannot please God. But ye are not in the flesh, but in the Spirit, if so be that the Spirit of God dwell in you. Now if any man has not the Spirit of Christ, he is none of his."

Some of you are now in relationships or marriages that are unequally yoked, which means you are in the wrong marriage. You know that you are only attracted to what this man has. Are you desperate? I am convinced that a man can tell when you are just desperate for "*a* man." He can tell by your standards, if you are broken or whole, an objective or subjective woman. There is something within you that keeps attracting just "*a* man." That means you need to check yourself. You see, God is trying to get you to see beyond the titles, material possessions, looks, education—anything outside of His will that can easily attract just "*a* man."

Do you remember me mentioning that I was seeking love impatiently in transition time after time—attracting "*a* man" and not "***the*** man"? I must admit. I was desperate at one point in my life. I did not want to be lonely, as so many women would probably say today. Some of us fail to realize that loneliness is only a state of mind. Once you have subjected yourself to "*a* man," you will later find yourself caught up in that "web of emotions." Some of you will stay in a comfort zone and accept the unacceptable.

Let us take this time to talk about "***the*** man." The man may be a pastor, minister, or he may be just a man that delivers pizza. He can drive an old car, and wear clothes less than what would attract your attention, even in need of a haircut or overdue shave. This does not mean based on your own desire that this is not "***the*** man."

Who is the man who God has purposed just for you? This man is the man who knows his position as a husband, leader—whatever his ordain position is. The man who will love you unconditionally! The man who submits to God! The man who receives his instructions from God, and not his friends! The man who understands and values your worth! The man who respects you! The man who honors you! The man who is faithful! The man who will provide! The man who will encourage you! The man who will honor his vows until death do you part! Mind you, I am not saying "***the*** man" has to be perfect, but let God handpick him for you because He knows your position as husband and wife. He knows that the foundation will be solid. He knows that the ministry will be mighty in Him. But He also knows that you are not just "a woman." Through prayer, fasting, meditation, and supplication, He knows that you are "the woman."

You will continue to find yourself repeating this same cycle until you surrender. Once you have surrendered, He will heal your brokenheart and make you whole. He will build a shield of protection around you, the kind of shield that will protect and guide you into the path of freedom so that you can no longer attract "*a* man," but instead "***the*** man," by becoming "the woman."

PRAYER:
Lord, I thank you for blessing me with "the man" and not just "a man." Help me to wait on you Lord, because I know that you will send him to me at an appointed time.

AFFIRMATION:
From now on I will practice patience daily and wait on you Lord. I will continue to motivate, encourage and tell myself that I am worthy of God's best.

CHAPTER 4

INTERCESSOR

"...The effectual fervent prayer of a righteous man availeth much."

(James 5:16)

I was on the prayer warrior team at my former church, and we interceded every Saturday morning for family members, friends, pastors, and others—in every area of their lives. I felt the power of God move as His presence filled that place with a fresh anointing each time we met. The anointing was so high that I could actually see spiritually what was happening in the midst of our praying. I have learned over the years that prayer is one of the greatest needs in today's society. Don't you agree? There is a formula that I have used, and it has worked for me; so, I believe it will work for you too. **Faith** plus **Prayer** equals **Power**.

PRAYER IS POWER

Prayer is directly speaking with God. That means you can share any thoughts, pains, joys, and so forth, all by opening your mouth and speaking to our Heavenly Father. Prayer is important, necessary, and a powerful privilege, all conducive to a healthy relationship with God and personal growth. By communicating with Him, your relationship with Him will grow, and it will allow you to be open in telling Him about your problems, asking Him for direction, and seeking Him whole-heartedly—through prayer? He has to be your first priority every day. When you pray continually throughout each day, it can increase the power within you. The power of prayer is truly an awesome thing. Having power allows you to defeat the enemy on every hand.

Just imagine talking to your earthly father about something that is been bothering you, whether its job related, a friend, or even your children acting up. If he loves you, he is going to offer support and comfort to help you get through it. Now how much more God loves you. How much more comforting can He be. He not only wants to help you get through your circumstances, but He wants to carry you through all of them. In 1 Peter 5:7 we read, "Casting your care upon him: for he careth for you." He is the comforter. So, are you broken? Are you hurting? Are you sad? Pray about it. Just like you can call your earthly father or other people to tell them about what you're going through, try calling God, no matter what time of day or night it is, He will answer.

You cannot make it without prayer. When there is a lack of prayer during trying times, the burden(s) of circumstances are often compounded. God did not say that you were not going to have trials, but faith and prayer can get you through them. Have you ever wondered why you cannot seem to shake whatever it is that may have you bound? Have you ever experienced having a weak prayer life? If so—don't stop praying! You should not put any limits on your prayer life. Paul and Silas proved that. The Bible says Paul and Silas prayed until the doors were opened. Here's their story:

Acts 16:25-26 says, "And at midnight Paul and Silas prayed, and sang praises unto God: and the prisoners heard them. And suddenly there was a great earthquake, so that the foundations of prison were shaken: and immediately all the doors were opened, and every one's band were loosed."

This story shows us the power behind prayer. God released them from behind prison walls. Now if God answered Paul and Silas's prayers, He will hear and answer yours. You, too, can be released from the prison walls of whatever it is that have you locked down (bound), in your mind that is. Many of us are in prison, right in their minds.

Here's another story: This one is about Hannah who prayed earnestly that God would heal her womb so that she could bear a son. 1

Samuel 1:12-15 says, "And it came to pass, as she continued praying before the Lord, that Eli marked her mouth. Now Hannah, she spake in her heart; only her lips moved, but her voice was not heard: therefore Eli thought she had been drunken. And Eli said unto her, How long wilt thou be drunken? Put away thy wine from thee: And Hannah answered and said No, my Lord, I am a woman of a sorrowful Spirit: I have drunk neither wine nor strong drink, but I have poured out my soul before the Lord."

After Hannah had lain out her troubles before the Lord, pouring her heart out, He gave her strength and opened up her womb so that she could conceive a child named Samuel. Can you remember the times that you have gone to God in prayer and poured your heart and soul out before Him? Didn't He answer your prayers?

God is so worthy of everything. Just like He answered Hannah, He will answer you too. Just go to Him with a sincere heart and made up mind. He is just that "big". He is a phone call away. He will give ear to your cry. He is definitely worthy of serving. I mean, He will turn everything around in a matter of seconds, minutes, or hours.

PRAYER:
Lord, I thank you for being a God that I can lay out my troubles before and you'll give ear to my cry. I thank you for understanding me, for you have made every part of me. You know all about me.

AFFIRMATION:
I will be consistent in my prayer life. I will pray in the morning. I will pray in the evening. I will pray at night. I know that I can receive from Heaven with prayer, fasting, faith, and obedience.

THE IMPORTANCE OF PRAYING FOR OTHER WOMEN

As women of God, we can help each other through our prayers. Many of us have experienced adverse circumstances that have become overwhelming and burdensome. Sometimes those circumstances, problems, and situations only need a touch of prayer. Ladies, we all know that we face some of the same issues in life. There is a great need for us to come together and pray for each other daily. We do not have to go through these circumstances of life by ourselves. We have each other. We need each other. Do not let jealously, envy, gossip, or strife stand in your way.

> *PRAYER:*
> *Lord, I first thank you for teaching me how to pray. Although I have had challenging times, I thank you for blessing me to make it through them all. I thank you for blessing other women to pray for me, even when I could not pray for myself.*
>
> *AFFIRMATION:*
> *I will pray for women on a daily basis to become whole in virtue.*

THE IMPORTANCE OF ASSOCIATION WITH OTHER WOMEN OF VIRTUE WHO WILL INTERCEDE

God allows women from all walks of life to cross each other's path. There is no limit to virtue—virtuous is who we are—or striving to become. One of my good friend's and prayer partner, Phyllis, mentioned earlier in the book, prays for me and with me. I pray for her too. Not only do we pray for each other, we pray for others. We both have experienced the power of God right through the midst of our praying. I can remember a time when I was facing a famine that lasted for well over six months, but in that season I needed a financial break-through within twenty-four hours. She and I prayed for about an hour or so. She told me not to fret because God was going to show Himself before the deadline. Sure enough, I started receiving financial blessings before midnight.

It does not matter how strong you are, you still need the prayers of the righteous. I know that individual prayers can be just as effective, but in Matthew 18:20 we read, "For where there's two or three gathered together in my name, there am I in the midst of them." When there are two or more people in agreement and believe by faith that God is going to bless, they too can experience what we had experienced—a miraculous move of God.

You can always find a prayer partner, a sincere woman or man of God who can pray for you, even when you cannot pray for yourself. There have been times when I could not even pray, but my friend would say, "God knows your heart, just moan if you have to."

PRAYER:
Lord, I thank you for placing women of God in my life who are sincere about the power of prayer. I thank you, Lord, that we can combine our prayer with faith and watch you move.

AFFIRMATION:
I will commit myself to finding a woman of God that will pray for me as I pray for her. I will make myself available even before sunrise.

THE IMPORTANCE OF PRAYING FOR GROWTH AND CONTINUED VIRTUE

It is important to pray for spiritual maturity, and in your virtue. As your relationship with God increases, you can walk in wholeness. Your daily aim should be to become more and more like Christ, and take on His character. So many of you are hindered because of the choices you have made. As I mentioned earlier, opening yourselves up to different unfruitful friendships and relationships can stunt your spiritual growth. Some people are not producing good fruit. In Matthew 7:16-17 we read, "Ye shall know them by their fruits? Do men gather grapes or thorns, or figs of thistles? Even so every good tree bringeth forth good fruit: but a corrupt tree bringeth forth evil fruit."

It is good to examine your friendships. If a friendship is not producing good fruit, then there is definitely a need to break away. That friendship can be with a male or female. Your concern should be only producing good fruit. Do not be afraid to let people go. Some people do not have any intentions of changing. They do not even have a desire to advance to another level in their life. Resisting change can have an impact on your growth, too. Have you ever been in a relationship that you recall being better off before you met that person? Have you ever experienced losing more in your involvement with that person than gaining? Has the person been critical of everything you have said or done? Simply, have you found yourself going in a backward motion instead of moving forward? These are the kinds of questions you need to ask yourself. Some people are just meant to be in your life for a "season," and some are not meant to be in your life at all. It is very important to know what a person represents, whether it is a friendship or a relationship.

PRAYER:
Lord, I thank you for continued growth. I thank you for everything that has happened in my life—the good as well as the bad. I thank you for allowing me to grow and learn from my mistakes and teaching me how to make better choices in life.

AFFIRMATION:
From this day forward, I will change my walk, talk, actions, and the motives of my heart. I will build my relationship with God and accept only His truth.

CHAPTER 5

RIGHTEOUS

"Rejoice in the Lord, O ye righteous: for praise is comely for the upright."

(Psalm 33:1)

We are the righteousness of God because He says we are. There is nothing that can stand in the way of who we really are. There is no sin, fault, or weakness that is greater than who you are in Christ. If you tell yourself daily that you are the righteousness of God, you are speaking words of life. He is the bread of life. He reigns from Heaven, knows all things, and is omnipresent. His omnipresence is your assurance that He is everywhere at all times; this means He is always with you. He can identify His own—His children.

A RIGHTEOUS WOMAN OF GOD

You are God's daughter. Just like a diamond ring, you can see the reflection of it from afar. It shines with a sparkling glow. It is a jewel that many women have desired at some point of their life. Well, God can see a reflection of Himself in you from afar. He can make and mold you into the woman of virtue, but you have to submit to His will and commit yourself into His hands.

God can exalt and anoint you to shine before nations, just like a diamond ring. This is to say, as a diamond can be seen among common rocks, you also will shine as a diamond among your family, community—everywhere you go. In 1 Corinthians 2:9 it states, "But as it is written, Eye hath not seen, nor ear heard, neither have entered into the heart of man, the things which God hath prepared for them that love him."

Sometimes you may fall short of His glory. No matter what you have done, He will forever love you. He is always there to receive every part of you. He can sustain you, even in your weakest hour. He will never let go of your hand because you belong to Him.

PRAYER:
Lord, I thank you for holding my hand and identifying me as your righteousness.

AFFIRMATION:
I will speak that I am His righteousness all the days of my life.

THE HONOR OF THE RIGHTEOUS

God will honor you when you honor Him. He loves to be honored. He does not want us to put anyone or anything before Him, not even our pastor. We should honor God in the mornings, evenings and at night—everyday! We show Him honor when we seek Him for our daily steps through prayer and by asking Him to order our footsteps. We also give God the glory when we accept His guidance, listen to His voice, walk in love, forgive others, and worship Him. Yes, we should acknowledge Him in all our ways!

You must continue to honor Him in your body, which is the temple of the Holy Spirit. In 1 Corinthians 3:16 it states, "Know ye not that ye are the temple of God, and that the spirit dwelleth in you?" This means you are a very precious gift, and so is your body. Once you realize who your body really belongs to and how you have been bought with a price, then you can look the enemy straight in his eyes and tell him, "No—I am not compromising myself—ever—I belong to God!" In 1 Corinthians 6:20, it states, "For ye are bought with a price: therefore glorify God in your body, and in your spirit, which are God's." Do you remember how I shared with you that the enemy, the devil, can come in any form? Yes, I am trying to convey that sometimes the devil makes our mom, dad, children, husband, or anyone else do evil things that they may not even know they are doing or maybe they do not know the devil is making them do these things. You should always think about God before you act. Your thoughts of Him are honorable.

> *PRAYER:*
> *Lord, I thank you for honoring me for my righteousness and obedience.*

> *AFFIRMATION:*
> *From this day forward, I will honor the Lord daily, in my walk, talk and in my lifestyle.*

WALKING UPRIGHT BEFORE THE LORD

God is *EL-Shaddai (*Almighty God). He wants you to walk before Him with an upright heart. He searches and reigns the heart of man. He does not look at the outer man, but the inner man. He can reach you when no one else can, so it is very important to get your heart right with God. You should ask God what kind of heart you have and He will show you. What you do for God is the only thing that is going to last—forever. In Proverbs 28:18 we read, "Whoso walketh uprightly shall be saved: but he that is perverse in his ways shall fall at once."

The Bible mentions several people who were upright including Job, Samuel and David. (David had an issue which I will share with you below), just to name a few. These were men who truly had a heart for God, and God found favor in them as well as others. Take a look at these few brief stories and you will see how these three men pleased God in some form. You will see how you can also find yourself walking in the same path these men walked in. Walking upright before God is not a matter of gender. It is a matter of a desire to live for, through, and in honor of our Heavenly Father.

Let me direct your attention to a story in the Bible about a man named Job. He was a perfect and upright man who feared God and deliberately stayed clear of evil. Satan sought Job. The devil knew that Job was upright, but the devil knew that Job feared God. What Job most feared came upon him though. But Job refused to take part in evil, even when his wife tried to get him to curse God, he refused to do it. Job went from being inconceivably wealthy to becoming dirt poor and losing his thriving business and how he enjoyed good health and then being stricken with chronic health problems. The Bible says, "Job was smote with sore boils from the sole of his foot unto his crown." He lost everything he had, including his children, his wealth, and his business – he lost everything!

Job's wife had always enjoyed their condition, and in coming to a new place in their life, she encouraged him to curse God and die, but he still walked upright before the Lord. His life was totally attacked and turned upside down by evil, yet he stood no matter what came his way. Everything he lost was restored to him a hundredfold. (I encourage you to read the Book of Job to learn more about this dynamic man).

There are some of us today who God has asked Satan the same question that He asked concerning Job, "Hast thou considered my servant _____," that there is none like her in the earth, a perfect and upright woman, one that feared God, and escheweth evil?" Don't fear, my friend, He knows exactly what it takes to make and mold you into the woman He desires for you to be. He knows how to operate on your heart.

Just because you may go through hard times as Job did, does not mean there is not glory on the other side. It would be fair to say that none of us would choose to go through severely challenging times, yet we would gladly admit that much of the strength, wisdom, and understanding we have gained in our life was in fact, afforded by making it through these times. By no other way would this book be possible.

David—another upright man—was a man after God's own heart. He was the one that Saul found favor in. He was the little shepherd boy who killed the philistine giant—Goliath (the enemy). (More information about David is provided in 1 Samuel 17 and the Book of Psalm, which was written by David).

Although David was an upright man, he had his own challenges. A moment of lust that led to adultery caused him a life of sorrow. The problem with this is the woman David lusted over was somebody else's wife. Even worse, David had her husband killed so that he could be with her. Therefore, he had blood on his hands. A baby was conceived through David's relationship with the married woman. This baby also had a problem, and died. David really loved this child, yet he had to bear the responsibility of his actions. There is no substitute for doing what is right, simply because it is right. The Bible says, "Now therefore the sword shall never depart from thine house; because thou has despised me, and hast taken the wife of Uriah the Hittite to be thy wife" (More information is available in 2 Samuel-Chapter 11, 12).

I am certain some of you might be saying, "What a harsh punishment?" But we should take a look at this story from a woman's perspective and bring home. Imagine you are saved, sanctified and you are filled with the Holy Ghost. You have a heart after God. You speak in tongues. You prophesy. You are shining before many. In sum, you are an upright woman.

But you seemed to have the same problem as David, and that is lusting after someone else's husband. Hmmm……Who are you? Who am I talking to now? Whose marriage have you broken up? Whose household have you taken money from? Whose husband has impregnated you? You might be saying, "But God is a forgiving God." And you are right. Yes, God is a forgiving God. And guess what? He forgives and He forgets.

Okay, but do not think just because you are a woman, you cannot face a great chastisement as David received. Do not think that you are exempt from the sword falling upon your home. Do not think that the iniquity cannot fall on your children. I do not mean to scare you, but this thing is real. We are living in a world that is governed by universal laws—you reap what you sow; what goes around comes around. This has been expressed in countless terms since the beginning of time. There is no escaping that which is inescapable.

The Bible goes a little further and tells us that a messenger was sent to David to basically tell him that someone would sleep with his wife before the sight of men, as he had slept with Uriah's wife. In 2 Samuel 12:11-12 we read, "Thus saith the Lord, Behold, I will raise up evil against thee out of thine own house, and I will take thy wives before thine eyes, and give them unto thy neighbor, and he shall lie with thy wives in the sight of this sun. For thou didst it secretly: but I will do this thing before all Israel, and before the sun." This is a perfect example of what went around came back around.

Have you or someone you know of been in a similar situation? You need to remember one thing—"...God is no respecter of persons..." (Acts 10:34). Do not think you are so holy that you cannot receive a whipping from God, because you will reap what you sow, and that law applies to everybody.

Samuel—he was one that God favored even before Hannah conceived him. He was already called and appointed to do what God had purposed him for. The Bible says, "He was established to be a prophet of the Lord" (1 Samuel 3:20). Samuel was an upright man, and he was obedient. Even until he became an old man, he was obedient to God's instructions. You see, he followed the instructions of the roadmap (God). He communicated to the house of Israel what God told him. Obedience has been a challenge for a lot of you, but I will talk about that later.

PRAYER:
Lord, help me work on my heart daily so that I will be able to walk upright before you so that you will be well pleased with me.

AFFIRMATION:
I decree to walk upright daily, in love so people from all walks of life will be drawn to you, Lord.

THE RIGHTEOUS WILL PREVAIL

Do not think for a minute you cannot win the race that is set before you. Do not think for a minute you cannot become successful. Do not think for a minute you cannot see yourself delivered and set free. Do not think for a minute you cannot take control over your thought process and change your way of thinking. Do not think for a minute you cannot raise healthy-minded children because you may have faced many challenges in your childhood. Do not think for a minute you cannot walk in love. Do not think for a minute you cannot forgive. Do not think for a minute you cannot become a virtuous woman. Do not think for a minute you are a loser. In Proverbs 23:7 we read, "For as a man thinketh in his heart, so is he…" If you think you can, you shall.

No matter what it is that you want to do or become in life, you should always remember that you are a winner, and you can prevail over any obstacle the enemy places in your path. You must continue to press your way through the many storms and challenges of life because they will come, especially when you are trying to move forward.

Remember to always put God first—before you start anything, even if it seems to be a difficult task. I know sometimes it can be a battle, but all the battles belong to Him. I want to remind you that Jesus fought a battle that has been already won for all of us. No enemy could stand up against Him. Just like the Father had Jesus' back, the Father also has your back. So, do not fret; just keep fighting until the end. Never forget this, God is with you. His righteous will always prevail over the enemy.

The Bible shares one of my favorite stories concerning a battle being fought and won by King David. Now David was the shepherd boy who stood up against Goliath, the obstacle most feared by the Philistine. But David proved through his faith, righteousness and strength that he could destroy Goliath. Besides, he knew God had already given him everything he needed to win the battle. He won the battle, and became king. You will find in reading about David that he had been faced with many obstacles during his young life, which he overcame, the foundation of his victory over the giant.

You need to ask yourself these questions: Who is your Goliath? Is it fornication? Is it drugs? Is it gambling? Is it gossiping? Is it depression? Is it oppression? Is it lying? Is it idolatry? Is it drunkenness? Is it adultery? Is it fear? Is it laziness? What is it? Which one of these sins is hindering your progress? You must face your Goliath before you can win the battle.

PRAYER:
Lord, I thank you for blessing me to run and win the race that is set before me. Lord, teach me how to fight with the Word that you have given me and the power that you have bestowed upon me.

AFFIRMATION:
I will continue striving to be the best that I can be and persevere until the end. I decree that I will keep fighting and press my way through my trials and tribulations because I know that I will soon prevail over any obstacles that I may face from this day forward.

CHAPTER 6

TRUTHFUL

"Pray for us: for we trust we have a good conscience, in all things willing to live honestly."

(Hebrew 13:18)

HONESTY is one the greatest values a person can ever have. You are open for correction and perfection when you are willing to be honest with yourself, with God, and with others. There have been a number of circumstances that have occurred which have caused some of you to be dishonest. Some of you are confined by negative past experiences, which seemingly drive you to a place of being dishonest in the smallest of matters. You have used those experiences to exonerate why you are not truthful at times. I had to use the three-fold confession, and that was first being honest with *self*, *God* and with *others*.

BEING HONEST WITH YOURSELF

The first person you have to be honest with is yourself. Although that could possibly be a challenge for some of you, nonetheless it is something you must do if you want to be free. How can you expect to overcome certain issues if you are living in denial? You cannot be afraid to admit that you are in a certain place in your life. If you have a problem with something, just admit it. By doing so, you will begin to feel a sense of relief. You see, many of us deceive ourselves time after time simply because of being dishonest with self. We are our biggest enemy!

Here is an example for you to think about: You have a problem with alcohol. You find yourself every single day craving beer or whiskey. Now, you are on your way to the store to buy a beer or two, maybe even a six pack (if you desire more) to satisfy that craving. It does not matter if it is a cheap beer or two; you just need something to quench the addictive thirst. This might be true for some of you, but do not feel bad because all of us deal with something on some level, whether it is fornication, gambling or adultery.

Looking on the surface, it is a bit obvious you are battling with alcoholism. Do you see this as being a problem in your life? Is this one of those obstacles standing in your way? "Well, I only drink one or two, but every now and again I'll drink a six or twelve pack," *now you're talking*, "but I don't get drunk." "I only drink when I'm angry." "I only drink when I'm going out for the night." *Oh boy, here are the excuses.* Now you are really in denial about this issue you have with alcohol. Everybody sees that this is a weakness for you, yet you have a hard time admitting the problem.

Let me reiterate what I mentioned earlier. You have to be willing to admit that you have a problem first, so that means you must be honest with yourself. Listen, God really wants to mature you. He wants to move anything that is hindering your growth completely out of your life, so that He can use you (the vessel) in a way that He is going to get the glory out of it.

PRAYER:
Lord, I thank you that I can be honest with myself. I thank you Lord for showing me my problems, mistakes and fixing every part of me that is broken, which has been causing me to act in a way that is contrary to who you have purposed me to be.

AFFIRMATION:
I decree to search deep within and pull out any hidden secrets, hurts, shortcomings, lies, and pain that are embedded in my heart and admit them, and then take them to God so that I can be free indeed.

BEING HONEST WITH GOD

Many of you have had a hard time being honest with God. You must be honest with Him because He already knows everything about us. In 1 John 1:9 we read, "If we confess our sins, He is faithful and just to forgive us our sins, and to cleanse us from all unrighteousness." He will cleanse you from self and the negative choices you have so freely made, causing you to go against His will. You remember me sharing that you must first admit (confess) you have a problem. When you open up to God, you give Him room to come in and repair the problem you are facing. You may be in a situation that you think is too difficult for God, but there is nothing He cannot handle.

When you began to trust that He will not judge you as man will judge you, then you will feel more comfortable in wholeheartedly taking your problems to Him. You will lean that His judgment is righteous. That means He does not base this on what you have done or said to others or what was done or said to you, but what it is based upon is God's will for thinking, speaking, and acting in accordance to His righteousness. He will not condemn you. In Roman 8:1 we read, "There is therefore now no condemnation in them which are in Christ Jesus..."

Why is there such difficulty to be honest with God? Our Heavenly Father loves when we are honest with Him. If we embrace wholeheartedly the need to be honest with Him, our need for direction, correction, and even protection will be graciously bestowed upon us.

For most of us, the number of reasons we do not and will not open up to God is because in some way we find our situation hopeless. We do not trust very easily. After all, at the root of much of our hurt and pain over the years is someone or quite possibly several individuals, who we trusted hurt us. These people range from authoritive figures such as parents, ministers, teachers, and others we associate protection and guidance with. These people are often the culprit in our not trusting Him when there has been a violation in trust. It is understandable not to be open and honest with those we cannot trust.

It seems as though the people who symbolized having our best interest at heart violated us; they broke our hearts. Trusting or confiding in others can be a no-go area for most people. Besides, oftentimes those we would confide in do not always have the wisdom, knowledge, and understanding needed in order to move us forward. Also, there is paralyzing fear that this person could share your concerns with others. There is even the thought that those who could bless us in our time of need as friends today—may not be available to help tomorrow. This is how brokenness drives our thoughts. Yes, we have legitimate reasons for not opening up; yet you should not allow yourself (or the enemy) to convince you that a closed mouth in brokenness will get fed the meat of wholeness.

> *PRAYER:*
> *Lord, I thank you for quickening my spirit. I thank you for being the God that will listen to me and not condemn me in my shortcomings. I thank you that I can come to you and confess all of my weaknesses.*
>
> *AFFIRMATION:*
> *I will confess my weaknesses daily to the Lord. I will trust Him whole-heartedly. I demand of myself to be honest with God because He knows all about me.*

BEING HONEST WITH YOUR HUSBAND

Wives, you must understand the value of truth. This, in and of itself, can cause your marriage to flourish, along with your being whole. You see, truth in honoring people with honesty, not only honors them, but yourself and above God. Anything that honors God, He honors.

There have been many marriages shattered because of dishonesty. Can this be as a result of your brokenness? Honesty is one of the main factors that hold a marriage together. So, ask yourself whether lying is worth destroying your marriage? Meditate on that question for a moment. Can you really think of the reasons you have to lie? Is your husband lying to you? Is he cheating on you? Is he disrespecting you? Is he calling you bad names? Is he fighting you? Are you acting this way because of fear? Be honest with yourself. Do you lie because it is the quickest way to get out of the marriage? Is it by choice or convenience? Is it because of something that happened in your past that has carried over in your marriage? You must be committed to total honesty. Again, you cannot truly move forward without it.

Some of you will lie about the small things. I will be the first to say that I have done this. I remember a time when I was dishonest with my first husband about how much money I spent while shopping. *Oh, I know I am getting somewhere now.* I had a bad addiction with shopping. My husband did not disagree with me going shopping, but I was spending money we needed from the household to go shopping. Guess what? My dishonesty caused us to get behind on bills. Now the aftermath of this one lie resulted in him having to work overtime to meet deadlines of bills that were due. You may have experienced something similar. There are a lot of you that like to shop. Am I right about it? I know you like the shoes, clothes, jewelry, down to the manicures and pedicures. You see, you can have these things as long as it will not affect your marriage or household.

More importantly, you should not have to lie to get these material things. As you can see, it is not healthy to lie, and it can cause your marriage to sink. These small lies, like how much you spent on something you wanted can be a greater impact than you lying about cheating on him...stop lying! Lying is something God hates. He hates a lying tongue. In Proverbs 6:16-19 we read, "These six things doth the Lord hate: yea, seven are an abomination unto him. A proud look, a lying tongue, and hands that shed innocent blood, an heart that deviseth wicked imaginations, feet that be swift in running to mischief, a false witness that speaketh lies, and he that soweth discord among brethren."

PRAYER:
Lord, I thank you for blessing me to realize the impact of being a dishonest wife. I thank you for showing me how this can have an impact even on my children.

AFFIRMATION:
I demand of myself a commitment to be open and honest with my husband from this day forward.

BEING HONEST WITH YOUR CHILDREN

We need to be honest with our children, even as it relates to our being broken—regardless of who or what caused this. Yes, there is a right season to share with them, but it definitely needs to be addressed—all you are doing is opening up the line of communication. By doing so, many blessings can come about. In Proverbs 20:7 we read, "The just man walketh in integrity: his children are blessed after him."

We need to keep in mind that the relationship with our children should not be one that is based on lies. You cannot build a godly relationship with your children on the foundation of a lie. Some of you are living a lie, so it is easy to lie to others about anything. This kind of relationship will cause division in the home. Has your child ever questioned you about a certain issue that you were dishonest about it? Have you ever taught your child to lie? Were you taught to lie growing up?

I can remember when my daughter was about 6 years old. I would tell her if someone called to tell them I was not at home. Yes, I told her to do this especially if it was the bill collector. Does that ring a bell? I must admit, I had a problem with lying, too. Sure enough, she did just as I said. It is funny how we tell our children, "Do as I say, not as I do." Then, when they do what we tell them, we are angry because the seed has been sown and it has flourished like a daisy flower. And now they end up lying to us—about anything.

Lying in my home became a problem. My daughter started lying to me and I could not get mad. I had to accept what I had done. I now share with her the importance of the seeds that we sow and how they will grow, especially if they are planted right—you reap what you sow! It is impossible to sow a watermelon seed and expect any other fruit or vegetable.

Once the seed of a lie (no matter what it is about) has been planted in them and it has been watered by opportunities of selfishness, it can place them in a position of where lying and dishonesty is convenient. They, too, become liars. They will even conceal certain issues they could face or have secretly dealt with in the past—without your knowledge—and you do not want this to happen. So, let us be honest with our children about everything, and let us not teach them to be dishonest.

PRAYER:
Lord, I thank you for blessing me to be honest with my children. I thank you, Lord, for giving them to me and trusting me to teach them to be trustworthy.

AFFIRMATION:
I will walk in integrity every day in my home, on my job and in my church.

CHAPTER 7

UNDERSTANDING

"For the Lord giveth wisdom: out of his mouth cometh knowledge and understanding."

(Proverbs 2:6)

IT is much easier to communicate and listen to others when you have understanding. You must also have a desire to understand others before this can take place. Some of us are too judgmental, jealous, envious, angry, and we also lack love. We often discount a person's abilities, talents, gifts, because we do not have the desire to understand them. On my journey I have come to realize that religion can often hinder us from even desiring to understand others. But one thing is for certain, you must gain understanding first, even when it comes to your being a wife, mother or friend.

HOW TO GET UNDERSTANDING?

You can increase your understanding when you pray, meditate, study, research, and read the Bible and other books. In Proverbs 4:5 we read, "Get wisdom, get understanding: forget it not; neither decline from the words of my mouth." Apart from studying, researching, and reading there is no other way to gain the understanding to become God's best in your community, school, job, home—and even when it comes to other people. There was no way for me to have made it this far without gaining some of the truths for myself.

I recently finished graduate school. I could not have made it through school if I had not applied myself to my studies. There were standards set by my instructors that as a student I had to meet. There is no difference with God. We are His righteousness, but there are godly standards that we must meet. You are held accountable based on your level of maturity, yet, we are all subject to the laws He has established, and we can be penalized for what we may or may not know. In 2 Timothy 2:15 we read, "Study to shew thyself approved unto God, a workman that needed not be ashamed, rightly dividing the word of truth."

> *PRAYER:*
> *Lord, I thank you for an increase in understanding. I thank you for giving me the courage to gain more understanding.*
>
> *AFFIRMATION:*
> *I demand of myself a commitment to increase in my studying, researching, and reading. I will continue to study the Word of God to show myself approved unto Him, and other inspirational books that can help build and encourage me, and increase my understanding.*

UNDERSTANDING YOUR POSITION AS A WIFE AND SUBMISSION IN THE HOME

> "Trust in the Lord with all thine heart and lean not unto thine own understanding."
> (Proverbs 3:5)
>
> "A wise woman buildeth her house: but the foolish woman plucketh down with her hands."
> (Proverbs 14:1)
>
> "It is better to dwell in the wilderness, than with a contentious and angry woman."
> (Proverbs 21:19)
>
> "A virtuous woman is a crown to her husband: but she that maketh ashamed is as rottens in his bones."
> (Proverbs 12:4)

I want you to think about the Scriptures mentioned above for a moment. Now ask yourself these questions: "Am I leaning to my own understanding in my marriage? Am I rotten to my husband's bones? Am I a contentious woman? Am I a virtuous woman or striving to become one?" You need to be honest with yourself.

You must submit to God first. Submission to God honors Him. You will find that it is easier to submit to and honor your husband, your position, and duties as a wife (helpmate) when you relinquish control over to God. (More information is available in Proverbs 31:10-31). He is the keeper of every home. The blessings flow down through the husband. Even the anointing can flow through the husbands. Keep in mind that being placed with "the man" God has purposed is always easier to submit to than "a man" of your own desire.

The Scripture shares that Sarai did not have a problem submitting to her husband, Abraham. She knew that her blessings were linked to him. Her obedience to God allowed her to submit willingly to her husband who was submitted to God. Granted, Abraham made mistakes, too; especially the incident regarding Pharoah. When in a threatening situation Abraham acted out of fear for his life and lied, stating that Sarai was his sister rather than admit she was his wife (Genesis Chapter 12). Sarai still obeyed and respected him. The Word of God says that she would call him Lord, but she knew that she was submitting to God all along.

Many of you have leaned toward your own understanding in the home. You are sometimes the cause for the home to crumble and fall to pieces. A house that is not built on a solid foundation will not stand. The enemy has dominated your thoughts about how the house should be operated by your husband, which makes it difficult for you to submit to his authority. You must be committed to staying in line as a wife.

Prior to marriage, most of us were independent. You have not been receptive to your husband's leadership because you thought he was not capable of making the right decisions for the family. It is true that some husbands may not always make the best decision for the family, but you must maintain your position. God will take care of the husband if he is not lining up with His will. As long as your husband seeks God's will, He will lead him. You should not disrespect your husband's ("the man") authority. You were made to be his helpmate. Many marriages are on the brink of divorce because there is, and has not been, an acknowledgement of the authority that God has imparted in the man of the home.

> PRAYER:
> Lord, I thank you for blessing me to become a submissive wife. I am thankful for your limitless grace and mercy in my life.
>
> AFFIRMATION:
> I decree that I will submit to my husband and honor him daily.

UNDERSTANING THE JEZEBEL SPIRIT...WHO WAS SHE...HOW YOUR LIFE CAN BE AFFECTED BY IT AND WHERE DOES IT COME FROM?

Ladies, some of us have or have had what the Bible describes as a Jezebel spirit. I know this is true because there was a time in my life that I was operating under this spirit, but I did not realize it. Many homes are run and ruined by this spirit. A woman who possesses this kind of spirit simply desires to wear the pants. As a woman, your place is to help build your home. In Proverbs 14:1 we read, "A wise woman buildeth her house..." The Bible also, tells us much about Jezebel. She was one who ruled her household with this dominating spirit. Ahab, her husband, was a king. She wanted him to worship her prophets, and not God's. (More information is available in 1 Kings –Chapter 21:5-25)

Even this type of spirit can stem from childhood brokenness. Just imagine growing up in a house where you observed constant abuse by someone who was very controlling. It did not matter if it was from your mother or father, the fact is, you observed this type of behavior, so you thought it was all right. Since you are all grown up, this spirit of control is now working against you.

This means that if this abuse was toward your mother (and even you), from the man (your father) who said he loved you, yet he called you bad names, took the money you worked for, cussed you out if you did not agree with him—what he did not realize is through his dominance, he was only creating a certain type of behavior that would spill over into your adulthood. Typically this is an issue that affects all your relationships, especially your marriage and your being a parent.

You have become a woman who feels as though you have to protect and defend your position through control. This spirit has caused you to manipulate your husband (as Jezebel did), speak disrespectfully and in a condescending tone to him. It has even caused you to lie for convenience to maintain control, even if it meant to throw four-year-old temper tantrums when you could not have your way. Not only is this plain, old selfish, but this is a form of witchcraft. You are attempting to control people through unrighteous methods. Nagging until you get your way is deceptive and it needs to end right now!

You need to ask yourself: *Do I have a Jezebel Spirit?* If so, this is not the right spirit to have because it is definitely an enemy to your virtue and God's plan for your life. You should not open yourself up to this type of spirit—ever. Instead, you should take on the spirit described in Galatians 5:22-23, "But the fruit of the spirit is love, joy, peace, longsuffering, gentleness, goodness, faith, meekness, temperance, against such there is no law." You can never forget the enemy is seeking whom he may devour, so he wants you to act out of character and in a way contrary to bringing forth blessings and bringing honor to God and your husband.

PRAYER:
Lord, I thank you for helping me to understand the nature of the Jezebel spirit. I ask you to help me to take authority over this controlling spirit I currently have. I want to be free from this spirit and submit my thoughts, words, and actions to you in your righteousness! Lord, help me to be all you have purposed so that

my husband can do the same. You are our God and Redeemer. You are the head of our lives and I submit to you.

AFFIRMATION:
I demand of myself a commitment to perform my duties as a wife and submit to my husband's leadership in the home as God has ordained.

UNDERSTANDING DESTRUCTIVE SUBMISSION... YOU DON'T HAVE TO SUBMIT TO IT

What is destructive submission? Are you submitting to any type of abuse? Are you tired of hearing apologies even though you do not see changes? Are you submitting to a controlling man? Well, ladies, I am hear to tell you that if you are submitting to any type of abuse, then I call it "destructive submission," and you do not have to continue submitting to this type of behavior. You must ask yourself, "Do I have to submit to this behavior" If so, why do you think you have to submit? Do you really think God wants you to submit to any type of abuse? If you think so, then you have got it wrong.

Ephesians 5:25-29 says, "Husbands, love your wives, even as Christ also loved the church, and gave himself for it; that he might sanctify and cleanse it with the washing of water by the word. That he might present it to himself a glorious church, not having spot, or wrinkle, or any such thing; but that it should be holy and without blemish. So ought men to love their wives as their own bodies. He that loveth his wife loveth himself. For no man ever yet hated his own flesh, but nourisheth and cherisheth it, even as the Lord the church."

If you are now married and you are submitting to a husband who is abusive and controlling, then you need to find out if he loves himself, and whether he is broken. The Bible clearly instructs your husband to love you as he loves his own body, meaning himself. How can he love you when he does not love himself? He cannot love you if he cannot love himself. This is totally contrary to the Word of God.

A husband who understands the institution of marriage will have a clear picture of God's purpose for his role. He will understand that he is no longer a separate being from his wife in a spiritual, mental or emotional sense—he is one with his wife. He is his wife, and his wife is him, so to speak. Both of you would have been united in Holy matrimony as ordained by God to enter into a life of oneness with Him and with each other.

Your husband will understand that it is God who has given him authority in his home. This does not mean that he assumes the position of a dictator, but is in the blessed position of living, honoring, and cherishing the gift that has been given to him—the gift being you! Your husband's authority is one of love. It is God's representation in your home and in your life not a substitute. God's will is not for you to be abused as a gift by what should be a gift. Abuse or control on any level is unacceptable.

Many women pray for answers concerning submission in their marriages. They seek answers on whether to stay or leave. They also ask whether or not they are married to "the man" God intended for them, yet when their prayers are answered, they wrestle with whether or not it is God who has spoken, or is speaking to them.

You need to establish a relationship with God before you establish one with any man. When a man controls your mind, that is to say, when he thinks for you, it makes it harder to receive the voice of anyone outside of him, including God. So if he abuses you, and tells you things like, "You better not leave; You better not tell anybody I hit you; or I hit you because I love you; I fuss and cuss at you because I love you; I am the head of this house, and so forth, you had better understand it is time to leave because this is "destructive submission." Think about it. You can actually die from abuse, especially physical abuse. Do you really believe God wants you to stay in an abusive marriage?

Many women have been beaten by their husbands, cheated on, cussed out numerous times, and criticized. But somehow they have stayed in these marriages for many, many years, accepting apologies and roses again and again, as a verbal means of, "I'm going to change and "I Love You." Change does not come from any other object than one submitted to God. This means it is not about the gifts of change in his hands—it is a desire for change in his heart.

God has shown you all along this man can't love you because he doesn't love himself. Answer these questions:

- Are you still broken?
- Have you ever thought about your husband being a broken vessel too?
- Does he recognize it?
- Does he want to be healed?
- Is he seeking any spiritual counseling?
- Are you all seeking counseling together?

PRAYER:
Lord, I thank you for teaching me the essence of godly living and the divine purpose of marriage. Thank you for teaching me that I do not have to submit to any type of abuse because you have clearly instructed in your Word for my husband to love me as he loves himself. I know you would not permit him to hit me, cuss at me, lie to me and cheat on me—abuse me in any way. I am your daughter and I know you love and want your very best for me. I will wait patiently for you in all matters. I will be still and surrender to your will.

AFFIRMATION:
I will self-examine my mind and heart to determine if I am really whole. I will work on me first, but I will not continue to submit to negative abuse. I will no longer let anyone but God control my thoughts. I am free from the bondage of abuse from this day forward.

UNDERSTANDING YOUR POSITION AS A MOTHER IN THE HOME

A mother has a strong position in the home. We are accountable for caring for our children. I am sure you have heard the cliché, "Charity begins at home and spreads abroad." The way your children act at home is usually how they behave in the public. We, as mothers, must set standards for our children. We also have to teach them how to abide by the rules and regulations in the home. Living a godly life is so important in the home, and this lifestyle should be carried out in the schools and around their friends. Your children seemingly pick up on the negative behavior before they will the positive behavior.

When your children see you disrespecting your husband or going from one man to the next (if you are single disrespecting yourself), they have less respect for you. You must carry yourself in a respectable way, and that is by respecting yourself in and out of their presence. Daughters tend to model after their mother, so there is a great need to represent integrity, respect, love, dignity, meekness, kindness, and joy in your home. You should also demonstrate this when you are absent from the home. Your children do not have to see what you do in order to be affected by your actions. In Exodus 20:5 we read, "Thou shalt not bow down thyself to them, nor serve them: for I the Lord thy God am a jealous God, visiting the iniquity of the fathers upon the children unto the third and fourth generation of them that hate me."

You should always keep a smile on your face when life's challenges seem to overwhelm you. As a single woman, I have had many challenges running my home, but it has been built on the foundation of Jesus Christ. Do you remember me mentioning earlier that there is nothing too hard for God? Well, I have gone through many trials and tribulations, but I have had to remain positive during these hard times. I had to remind myself that God had something better for me, and He wanted to get the glory out of my circumstances. I had to encourage myself each time. I would even encourage my children to pray along with me. What we are faced with as parents affect our children. We are spiritually connected to them. We must be open to gain their thoughts and allow them to express themselves—out of the mouth of babes. In Matthew 21:16 we read, "And said unto him, Hearest thou what these say? And Jesus saith unto them, Yea; have ye never read, Out of the mouth of babes and sucklings thou hast perfected praise?"

Living a life pleasing to God benefits the entire family. If we lead in truth—truth will follow. That's to say, that if we raise a child in the way he or she should go, they will grow that way because it's the will of God. We must include our children in our relationship with God and encourage their own relationship with Him.

I considered it a blessing that God would have chosen me to go through and allow my children to be a witness to His strength within me. It was a blessing that they could relate to some of the ups and downs that life may present to them as they mature in the Lord. Through my tribulations, they were able to gain a closer walk with God, and it increased their prayer life.

PRAYER:
Lord, I thank you for my being able to perform my duties as a mother.

AFFIRMATION:
From this day forward, I will be consistent with using my mothering skills and the wisdom of God to raise my children to be well-balanced, healthy-minded children that will think soberly, read, study, pray, and most of all establish a relationship with God.

CHAPTER 8

OBEDIENT

"If ye be willing and obedient, ye shall eat the good of the land."
(Isaiah 1:19)

DISOBEDIENCE demands a price none of us can afford to pay. There is no amount of money that can be offered unto God for your obedience to Him. We cannot buy Him. Obedience is something you must offer to God. He cannot and will not do it for you. Walking in obedience is not what you do—it is who you are. Whatever you are becomes your lifestyle.

OBEDIENCE IS BETTER THAN SACRAFICE

In Hebrews 10:26 we read, "For if we sin willfully after that we have received the knowledge of the truth, there remaineth no more sacrifice for sins."

There is a story about Saul and his disobedience to God. God sent Samuel to anoint Saul to be King over His people, over Israel, and to obey God's voice in leading His people. Saul had his own agenda, as so many of us today. He wanted to do things his way. In sum, God had rejected Saul from being King. It is not about you. By now you should get the hint that it's all about God—not us! (More information is available in 1 Samuel-Chapter 15)

The Spirit of the Lord had departed from him. After reading this passage of Scripture, you will find that it is important to walk in obedience so that you can receive prosperity, in every area of your life. There is no need for any of you to lack in the blessings because of disobedience. I have found that it is better to receive the blessings for being obedient rather than God's mercy and grace for being disobedient.

I have been on both sides of the fence, living a life of disobedience and obedience or a combination of both. Hot...Cold...Lukewarm...well, my lifestyle at one point fitted them all. You remember me sharing the story of my second marriage. That was a prime example of a time in my life when I was walking in disobedience. I heard a voice, "D*o not do it!"* but I did it anyway. Just like Saul, I have even experienced doing the total opposite of what God's Word and the Holy Spirit instructed me to do. As a result, I could not receive any blessings. I felt as though the sword was in my house, just as I had earlier shared the story of David. I was totally out of God's will.

I was all by myself. As stated before, I had my own agenda. I thought that I was doing the right thing, but in essence, I was only deceiving myself by justifying the reasons I thought my actions were right. Living a life of disobedience can, in fact, lead to many adverse circumstances. These situations can be invited into your life through disobedience.

Disobedience to God gives the enemy legal right to come in and make your life miserable. He will take control of your thoughts by making you think what you are doing is acceptable, even though you are acting out of character as a child of God. Mind you, the enemy does not need the signature and/or approval from the judge on a physical level; this is strictly on a spiritual level. The manifestations of the impact of disobedience could possibly affect your life.

Here is an example. A husband and wife decide to divorce because of infidelity in their marriage. The end result is that both receive a divorce decree with the judge's signature, declaring they are no longer married This marriage started out with God as their foundation, which was built upon by their obedience. Slowly this started to fade. One spouse's mind was opened to the thought of sin, which progressed to full-blown sin, and resulted in infidelity. When one spouse sins, it affects the other! To cover up for betrayal, lies were offered instead of truth, when confronted by the innocent spouse. God was rewarding the truth in this matter to save it, but because the spouse was caught in selfishness and pleasures, the end result was divorce. Here is how it transpired: disobedient thought; disobedient action; disrespected marriage; denial of that action when discovered by the innocent spouse on a physical or spiritual level or a combination of both (meaning there was suspicion and then evidence—deliberate attempt to gain truth); further denial; distrust and divorce.

This again, started out with love and respect for each other. They had a fruitful marriage—the kind every couple desires to have and more. The woman decided to invite another man in her world. Her actions and motives led her to partake in adultery. Now she has given the enemy legal right to come into their home and do whatever he pleases. The harvest of this act can lead to separation, divorce, emotional hurt and pain, loss of trust, disrespect, broken children, failing health, loss of anointing, and so much more.

There is no such thing as fair game when you have given the enemy legal right to come into your life. The enemy never plays fair. In John 10:10 we read, "The thief cometh not, but for to steal, and to kill, and to destroy..." He will never warn you about his motives and intentions. He will use you and turn around and destroy you. He can never tell you anything about your future. He can never tell you the truth.

The enemy is a liar and will forever be a liar. He is a deceiver and a manipulator. He has no part in joy, peace, love, happiness or obedience. Just like the judge has the authority to give a criminal the minimum or maximum punishment for committing a crime, Satan also has the authority to kill, steal and destroy when we give him legal rights through disobedience to God. Disobedience to God is obedience to Satan.

PRAYER:
Lord, I thank you for having grace and mercy on me when I did not walk in obedience. I thank you for giving me the opportunity to walk in total obedience and receive your limitless blessings.

AFFIRMATION:
I demand of myself a commitment to walk in total obedience to God on a daily basis. I will make sure my lifestyle is consistent with the Word of God. I will not deceive myself in believing a lie and yield to the temptations of this world.

BEING BLESSED THROUGH OBEDIENCE

I will be the first to tell you about the blessings you can receive for your obedience. I can remember when I was involved in a previous adulterous relationship which I mentioned earlier. I was not yet divorced, but I had proceeded in another relationship. My life was contrary to His Word and His will for my life. Through recognizing disobedience, I was able to break free and experience a life of obedience. This was not easy; I had to go through some things and face some harsh consequences, but I made it! Once I made the choice to serve God with an obedient heart, things started to turn around for me. I started to experience one blessing after another. There has been no limit to what He has done for me. I thank Him most for grace and mercy; for His chastisement out of love; for not giving up on me; and for opening my eyes so that I could see through His eyes. I thankful for the spiritual gifts that have been bestowed upon me that have grown by leaps and bounds when I submitted to Him in obedience!

The blessings are entitled to all of His people. You should want to stay in His presence and walk in obedience so that you may continue to receive His "limitless" blessings. There are many women today who receive an abundance of His blessings. Walking in obedience is a part of God's plan for all of our lives as His beloved daughters.

To inherit the goodness of God's glory, and even just to experience a peak of His glory, is so amazing. You may have to go through some of the most challenging trials because of your obedience to God. You might suffer persecution for walking upright, but do not fret because you are walking for God. To meet these challenges by faith and knowing once you make it through you will be stronger, wiser, more caring, and loving—to the glory of God will be your reward. Reward comes after reasons to be rewarded. Those challenges that seem too much to bear will soon bow down to our strength, perseverance and faith when we take a stand for obedience.

PRAYER:
Lord, I thank you for my obedience. I have learned through my

obedience that the fruit is plentiful. I thank you for daily giving me the abundance of your blessing daily. I thank you for my life, health, strength, joy and love.

AFFIRMATION:
I will continue to walk in obedience daily. I will continue to speak blessings over my life and remain positive, even when things do not seem to line up to how I would like. I believe every day will present to me new blessings.

RAISING OBEDIENT CHILDREN

In Ephesians 6:1-3 we read, "Children obey your parents in the Lord: for this is right. Honour thy father and mother; which is the first commandment with promise: That it may be well with thee, and thou mayest live long on the earth." These Scripture were important to me because I was able to share them with my children. I instructed my children to read these Scripture daily as a foundation and guide to the road of their own obedience. Children face as many obstacles as adults. Parents often punish their children for being disobedient. You may restrict them from watching TV, going shopping, or even going over to their friend's house. Seemingly, whatever is enjoyable to them is usually what you find yourself taking away from them and this is because they did not uphold the standards you know are in their best interest as well as your best interest. This is how God sees us—as His children.

You can never blot out the issues that they have as children though. You must continue to share the Word of God with them and you must instill in them the rewards they can receive for being obedient; not only from you, but also from the spiritual rewards and blessings they can receive from our Heavenly Father.

You have an influence on your children, so they need to see you obey God. You are their example. Now, only you know if you are the best. You can either have a positive or negative impact on them. The principles you raised them by are usually the same principles they will use when they become adults and start their family. If you teach your children about God, and the importance of obedience, they will walk in faith and teach their children by their examples.

PRAYER:
Lord, I thank you for blessing me to raise my children in obedience and the admonition of you. I thank you that they are kind, respectful, happy, loving and trustworthy.

AFFIRMATION:
I decree that I have blessed children, and their children, and generations to come. The blessing will flow from generation to generation. They will continue to walk in obedience.

CHAPTER 9

UNCOMPROMISING

"Let your moderation be known unto all men. The Lord is at hand."

(Philippians 4:5)

TO compromise simply means to "agree or settle." When you come to a place in your life that challenges you to shift to a settling mode (being in a comfort zone) because it feels right, usually there is more than what appears to be real on the surface. In some instances, those things that seem right are often fabricated because of selfish desires, and this causes us to compromise with what has been presented to us—what we believe to be God sent. These desires can come in the form of a job, husband, car or house. These are common human desires we tend to seek and pray for. We must understand that anything contrary to God's will or His Word is not of Him.

THE WORD OF GOD IS UNCOMPROMISING

I would first like to share with you the importance of the Word of God. His Word is definitely uncompromising. It is like a two-edged sword. It can destroy the yokes of bondage. It should not be misinterpreted. It can bring healing and delivering in your lives. It can shine light on all the dark areas of your lives, including your brokenness. It is a blessing to receive the Word of God. In John 1:1-3 we read, "In the beginning was the Word, and the Word was with God, and the Word was God. The same was in the beginning with God. All things were made by him; and without him was not anything made that was made."

PRAYER:

Lord, I thank you for giving me your Word as a living principle for my life. I thank you that I can share your Word with my friends, family and my enemies.

AFFIRMATION:
I will receive your Word daily in my heart so that I can apply it to my life and every situation that present itself to me.

DO NOT KEEP COMPROMISING...KEEP YOURSELF UNTIL MARRIAGE

Marriage is honorable in God's sight. You should not have to feel pressured by any man to open up yourself to fornication. Fornication can defile the body. In 1 Thessalonians 4:3-5 we read, "For this is the will of God, even your sanctification that ye should abstain from fornication: That every one of you should know how to possess his vessel in sanctification and honour; not in the lust of concupiscence, even as the Gentiles which know not God."

Many of you have been in transition since your first relationship. The key to your ultimate happiness, peace and healthy self-esteem is finding and loving yourself, and becoming complete in God while you are a single lady. You do not have to feel like you are alone. Again, it is in your mind. Your mind can take you anywhere you want to go, but ladies, do not let the loneliness of mind take you in the bedroom to lie down with anyone other than your husband. "The man" is worth waiting for. If you want the best, you must strive to become God's best. You are precious and valuable, and your body is the temple of God.

Until God send you "your man," God is all you need. God will bring forth the groom ("the man") to you when you are ready. Remember, even when you think you are ready, there may be some areas He wants to work on in your life which are essential to fulfilling His purpose through your marriage. Also, because you are a jewel to God, you must remember that He is also getting your man (husband) ready for you. Be patient. Focus not on who your husband will be, or when he will show up. Trust God and keep moving forward and growing.

PRAYER:

Lord, I thank you for giving me the strength and power to remain abstinent until marriage. I thank you for giving me the wisdom to know the importance of abstaining from fornication.

AFFIRMATION:
I decree that I will save myself until marriage. I will remain Holy in my body. My actions and motives will be consistent with the Word of God concerning marriage. I will wait to give myself only to the husband that God has ordained for me. I will not allow myself to be tempted by appearance, looks, money, cars or any material thing that the world has to offer me.

COMPROMISING YOUR VALUES CAN BE AN ENEMY TO YOUR DESTINY

Some women find themselves compromising their values for many different reasons. Your values may be integrity or dignity, but do not compromise your values. Some of you have taken the Scripture, "God will give you the desires of your heart" literally. You have not comprehended what that Scripture really means. God does not give you something that is contrary to His Word. Do not think because you desire something so badly that you should accept anything that is presented to you. I do not care what it is—if it is not of Him, it is no good for you. If you are one of those women in the accepting mode, then you have clearly got it wrong. It is time to change gears, set standards, be patient and let God lead you on your daily path. Keep your mind focused on doing what is right. You could not even imagine what He has in store for you when you are doing what is right. He has so much for you, but you must remember that you have an assignment that you must first complete. God wants you to be happy on your journey, but remember happiness comes from within.

I have learned that many of us have compromised our godly morals and values because of our lack of understanding. It is not uncommon for some of our values to be confused or distorted because of our upbringing, or negative experiences, which lead to brokenness. But do not continue to compromise your values no matter what ungodly opportunity looks or feels like. You are God's own—a virtuous woman and you were born with a purpose.

PRAYER:
Lord, I thank you for blessing me to realize how valuable I am to you as a woman. Help me to stand on your Word and not to compromise my values under any circumstance.

AFFIRMATION:
I will no longer compromise my values. I demand of myself respect, honor, integrity and healthy thinking.

CHAPTER 10

SENSITIVE

"Bear ye one another burdens, and so fulfill the law of Christ."
(Galatians 6:2).

WE are truly living in a world that is full of insensitive people—those who cannot discern sensitive matters because of their lack of desire and love. Selfishness seems to surround us. Many people are too selfish to even step outside of themselves to even attempt to help those who have a need. The love has now waxed cold. (More information is available in Matthew 24:12)

KNOWING HOW TO BE SENSITIVE...BEAR YOUR SISTER'S BURDEN

Have you ever been burdened down, and went through life feeling like you have not had anyone to confide in—not your sister, friend or church member? Have you wanted to hold everything that was bothering you inside because you were too embarrassed to share it with anyone because you thought people would criticize you? Have you ever heard people gossiping after you shared your problems? If so, what kind of things have you heard them say? Was it, "I wonder why she's going through so much?" "She must be sinning!" "She has been looking so pitiful!" or "She needs to do better for herself!" "Have you heard?" "She is about to lose her car!" "She is about to be evicted!" "She has been fooling with that old sorry man!" How did all of this make you feel? Did you feel like people were being sensitive to what you were going through or being judgmental?

The truth is women find themselves trying to analyze why our sisters have so many challenges in their lives. Seemingly, when we know for sure, we yield to the spirit of gossip. By doing so, however, we are not being wise and loving, but instead we are being judgmental. What is most humbling is to realize that you may know where you have been and where you are right now—but you do not know what the future holds. Do you realize that you could find yourself in this person's shoes—or worse? At any given time, we can find ourselves in a terrible storm of life, whether due to a bad decision, mistake or just a trial as part of the human experience.

Having an ear to God's voice will allow you to discern the truth about your sister's circumstance, so that you are sensitive and not insensitive. God will lead you into all truth. He will direct your path if you allow Him in your life. He is a God of compassion. We are made in His image, so that means we, too, can possess His characteristics. God looks at our heart. What is in the heart is what will come out of the heart. If compassion is there, then it is impossible for you to be insensitive to what your sister or anyone else is going through in their life.

To be compassionate means to be sensitive. Below are some steps for you to learn and improve your skills for being sensitive to others:

1. Open your heart to receive God and let Him cleanse you from your ways so that you can operate with His heart, love, compassion and sensitivity.
2. Let go of your selfishness—it is not about you—it's about our Heavenly Father.
3. Confess daily that you are free from self and you can and will walk in Love.
4. Pray for discernment so that you can recognize sensitive matters.
5. Do not set limits on what you can do for others when God has blessed you to help others.

In 1 John 3:17 we read, "But whoso hath this world's good and seeth his brother have need, and shutteth up his bowels of compassion from him, how dwelleth the love of God in him?" I believe once you understand the dynamics of giving, you will become sensitive to sensitive to matters that require compassion.

PRAYER:
Lord, I thank you for Blessing me to walk in love. I thank you for allowing me to recognize sensitive matters and for guiding me through your spirit to helping others who are at a point where they cannot help themselves. I thank you Lord for blessing me to recognize that you are not a respecter of persons. I do not take for granted that I, too, can face a famine any day, even if it's because of a bad decision I have made.

AFFIRMATION:
From this day forward, I will walk in love and be consistent with my giving daily. I will ask of you Lord, what is it that you will have for me to do this day to be a blessing in the life of someone else.

BEING JUDGMENTAL CAN PREVENT BEING SENSITIVE

When you have a heart of compassion, it is easier for you to be sensitive without finding reason to judge another woman, or anyone. You may not be able to help this other woman in the way she needs it, but you can share with her that her circumstances are not a match for God and faith. Share with her that God loves her, and He has a reward for her if she presses her way through the fiery trials. Share with her the importance of her standing still so that she may see the salvation of our Lord, and gain direction and understanding.

Some of you may be going through this right now. You may be in a pit, raising your hand for help, hoping someone would pass by and help. Imagine it. Put yourself in somebody else's shoes right now. Imagine you are in a pit and everybody is passing you by. Your hand is reached out as far as it can go. People can barely see it because you are sinking. You are yelling for help. You have seen people pass by on both sides of this pit. You have noticed family members, friends and church members—no one is stopping. There have been those who noticed you, but they do not stop. You can hear some of those who are passing by, saying, "Did you hear about so and so, she has not been doing good?" You know, she is hungry; she has been begging. She does not have any money to pay me back if I help her. She does not even pay her tithes, so why should I help?" But all you need is for someone to be sensitive enough to pull you up. Do not worry about feeding me, just grab my hand. Do not look at what I have done, just grab my hand. Do not look at my past, just grab my hand. Just hold on my sister, your angel is on the way! God's got your hand! He will send the right person by—the Angel that is not going to look at your past or throw stones at you.

The Bible tells us about the story concerning the Good Samaritan, which I have found to be so profound. This story shows that everyone you think should help you is not always in a position to help because they are too judgmental, selfish or insensitive. Or, it could be that God has redirected these people because it could be His will for you to be where you temporarily are. Let me pause for one moment:

Luke 10:30-34 says, "And Jesus answering, said, a certain man went down from Jerusalem to Jericho, and fell among thieves, which stripped him of his raiment, and wounded him, and departed, leaving him half dead. And by chance there came down a certain priest that way: and when he saw him, he passed by on the other side. And likewise a Levite, when he was at the place, came and looked on him, and passed by on the other side. But a certain Samaritan, as he journeyed, came where he was: and when he saw him he had compassion on him. And went to him, and bound up his wounds, pouring in oil and wine, and set him on his own beast, and brought him to an inn, and took care of him."

Think about this parable. Can you even begin to fathom this story? Are you that friend, family member, or church member that probably would judge a person where he or she is was in their life? In Luke Chapter 10 verse 25, there was a certain lawyer who wanted to know how he could inherit eternal life. And Jesus responded by giving this parable. In essence, Jesus was saying, "Just help your neighbor."

The Good Samaritan gave and he was sensitive to what had just happened to the man. He did not make any excuses not to help, such as "I'm on my way to church," or "I'm on my way to a meeting." We must realize that God shows up when our heart is in the right place. Remember, Jesus' ministry was not about going into the church. He rarely went to church. So we can still bless on our way there. Most associate giving with money and find every reason not to be a blessing in someone's life. There are many ways to give. I have come to understand that if you have a heart of compassion and in the mode of giving all the time, you will be more alert when God is telling you no—not this time.

I can remember in March 2006, I was faced with multiple challenges as mentioned earlier, that forced me in what I called "the pit of purification"—a pit that would ultimately lead to my purpose—a new anointing—a new "level" in God. It seems as though when I was in the pit I was being buried further by the tongues of many who I thought would have been sensitive. That included family members and church members. I am certain each of you can identify with some situation you were in, and there were some family members, church members, and friends who simply spoke against your decisions, past, or some other experience. They could not fathom what God was doing in your life, nor could they see the strength and love you had during your storm.

I now realize that when I was in the pit, God used that situation to shake, make, bake, mold, develop and increase the passion of my purpose. You see, while I was in the pit, I heard a word from the Lord, "There is therefore now no condemnation in them which are in Christ Jesus." It is so amazing to me that when you are going through the darkness and you think that you are all alone, God will never leave you, nor will He forsake you.

Shortly after, God gave a Prophetess at my former church a powerful Word from the Most High. One Sunday morning right before worship service, she stood up before the congregation and said that God gave her a "Word" to communicate with the church. She told us to turn to the book of James and read along with her, chapter four verses, eleven and twelve: "Speak not evil one of another, bretheren. He that speaketh evil of his brother and judgeth his brother, speaketh evil of the law, and judgeth the law: but if thou judge the law, thou art no a doer of the law, but a judge. There is one lawgiver, who is able to save and to destroy: who art thou that judgest another." You may find yourself wearing the shoes of being judgmental right now. Do not be afraid to ask about a situation rather than judge it.

I am now convinced that many people have suffered much pain and have been deeply hurt as a result of someone being insensitive to them while in the pit. There have been many led by God to help, but they refused to help because they set limits on what they could not do, instead of what God could do through them. God holds all the blessings. He just needs willing vessels to channel His blessing through. "We are blessed to be a blessing." It is important that we stop judging people.

PRAYER:
Lord, I thank you for teaching me to be sensitive and not judgmental.

AFFIRMATION:
I demand of myself a commitment to start seeing people the way God sees them, in spite of the mistakes and choices they've made. I will pray for people daily.

BEING OVERSENSITIVE

Being oversensitive can create problems for you as well. There are simply times that God's chastening is in effect for you. This means He wants to teach make, mold and purify you—and bring total deliverance to your life. God can develop someone's purpose. There are also times when the enemy will use someone to cause you harm. If you would keep an open mind and heart, you will know when God is steering you away from being sensitive in a manner that could have a negative impact on you.

Here is an illustration of someone's purpose: Have you seen the movie, *The Passion of Christ?* I am certain that if you did watch it, then you shed many tears during and after the movie. You were probably sensitive and angry about how Jesus was treated. Your sensitivity would have probably made you fight for Jesus, even die for Him at that point in time. Do you remember when Jesus was carrying the cross and how people tried to help, but they were told to get back? They were very sensitive. But the reality is, He was **PURPOSED** to go through this fiery trial. His purpose was to die for us—for the remission of our sins. No one could have played the role Judas played in Jesus' life. Judas played the role of the villain in Jesus' life. This was hurtful to the people who loved Jesus, yet this had to take place. This was the Father's will. All this led Jesus to the cross to take our place there.

Through all the pain and suffering Jesus had to endure, His life taught us how to love, be sensitive, kind, tender, compassionate and caring. Nonetheless, we cannot let being oversensitive get in the way of God's purpose. Although the enemy treated Him so terribly, Jesus still showed the one thing He commands us to do—and that is to LOVE. Right before He commended His Spirit to God, Jesus said, "Forgive them for they know not what they do." (Luke 23:34). Many people struggle with forgiveness. In this instance, this was all about God's purpose. You may be going through circumstances right now for your purpose. I encourage you, sister, to continue praying and go through it. God's got you! Do not worry about the people who are talking about you. They really are being more of a blessing to you because their actions are pushing you toward your **purpose.**

Here is an illustration of the enemy using someone to cause hurt to you. Imagine you are a single mother striving to live right and take care of your children. You are doing well for the most part. You have joy, peace, patience, and money in your pocket—all the things to live a comfortable life on earth. But you have been lured into a relationship stemming from being oversensitive. Perhaps, you have a male neighbor who does not have a car and needs a ride to the store. He has told you that his children are hungry. You have decided to give him a ride because you are sensitive to his needs. The next day, he knocks on your door and asks you to give him a ride to a friend's house. The next day, he needs a ride to the mall. The next day, he needs to borrow money. Now this is becoming a problem, don't you think?

You are feeling sorry for your neighbor because you are looking at the fact he has children to feed, so with this in your mind, he could possibly be a provider. You fail to realize, however, there is more to being a man than just him being a provider. You are probably saying to yourself, "At least he is taking care of his family. He really needs a push. Everyone does not have a car. He looks good. He is probably a church-going man." You have found all the reasons to attach yourself emotionally to this man and justify your position to help him.

I use this example because the enemy has used your emotions time after time, and you have yielded to this kind of temptation for "a man." I was one of these ladies who fell into this trap. You may have found yourself feeling sorry for some healthy man who is able to work but simply refuses to. You have not been able to discern the darkness in him because you are too sweet, too sensitive, or broken, trying to find yourself. Because of your emotions, you can truly invite trouble in your life. If you are asking, "Is it wrong to have emotions?" The answer is, "No." God gives you emotions, but you can't confuse emotions with being oversensitive to a matter.

You might be in this place right now. Do not let being oversensitive cause you to be a foolish woman. Some people are creating their own pits simply through their negative choices. They are not being robbed of everything they have, like the man that fell among the thieves, and he was helped by the Good Samaritan. These people are actually mismanaging their resources by throwing them all into a bag with a hole in it. They are obviously not putting their money (and other blessings) to good use. In a case like this, you had better be very careful not to cast your pearls to swine—do not sow your goods (money, time, etc.) on bad soil because nothing is coming back. The enemy does not use any new tricks. He uses the same tricks over and over. He is roaming the earth seeking who to devour. All the enemy needs, is for you to yield to the temptations he presents to you.

PRAYER:
Lord, I thank you for giving me the heart to be sensitive. I thank you for allowing me to recognize when I am being oversensitive. I thank you for redirecting my path when the enemy tries to lure me in the direction of harm to me or my family.

AFFIRMATION:
I demand of myself to watch as well as pray. I will use the discernment that God has given me to recognize sensitive matters that are not to be touched.

RECIPROCAL SENSITIVITY

In Luke 6:31 we read, "And as ye would that men should do to you, do ye also to them likewise."

Many people take this Scripture out of context. I have found that most people pick and choose Scriptures to justify their position, whether their position is right or wrong. We must remember we cannot change the Word of God the way we want it. At one point in my ignorance I thought that if someone treated me wrong, I had the right to treat him or her the same way. It was not how they treated me but how I should have treated them that mattered. God judges based on what is right and not what appear to be right. People often play tit for tat and this is wrong. In Matthew 5:44 we read, "But I say unto you, Love your enemies, Bless them that curse you, do good to them that hate you, and pray for them that despitefully use you, and persecute you."

Some of you are sensitive, but you have held on to how someone has wronged you. In other words, you probably have not forgiven the person or people who hurt you. You have allowed whatever that issue was to prevent you from positively reciprocating, but instead you reciprocated negatively. I know that it is not easy to forget how a person has treated you, but you must continue to walk in love. You have to understand that some people just do not know how to act. They know that you have given and helped them before, but in essence they do not know how to give or be compassionate to you and others. They also could just be selfish. You have to continue to pray for those who simply just don't know.

PRAYER:
Lord, I thank you for letting me see others through your eyes. I thank you Lord for Blessing me to not look at their faults, but their needs. I thank you Lord for hearing my prayers concerning those who seemed to have a hard time reciprocating. Help them Lord to see the importance of being a blessing to others, as others have been to them.

AFFIRMATION:
I demand of myself to treat others the way that I want to be treated.

CHAPTER 11

WISE

"Whoso is wise, and will observe these things, even they shall understand the loving kindness of the Lord."

(Psalm 107:43)

YOU are now in a season that requires you to ask Almighty God for wisdom. You do not know if you are going or coming. Everything around you seems to be falling apart. The enemy has been presenting so many thoughts that you have been on the verge of yielding your vessel because it feels so much like God. Your family has turned their backs on you. The members of the church do not understand your pain and hurt. You do not have many friends. Your job demands you are in the office no matter what you are going through. You are at a crossroad in your life right now, and you need the wisdom to make a sound decision. Wisdom is a powerful gift.

HOW TO POSESS WISDOM...GOD GAVE IT TO YOU...SO USE IT

Wisdom comes from God, and it is given generously. You can possess wisdom by asking God for it. Some were born with wisdom and others have gained wisdom through their own personal experiences. You are to use wisdom to God's glory. In Proverbs 8:11 we read, "For wisdom is better than rubies, and all the things that may be desired are not to be compared to it."

2 Chronicles 1:6-12 says, "And Solomon went up o thither to the brazen altar before the Lord, which was the tabernacle of the congregation, and offered a thousand burnt offerings upon it. In that night did God appear unto Solomon and said unto him. Ask what I shall give thee. And Solomon said unto God, Thou has shewed great mercy unto David my father, and hast made me to reign in his stead. Now, O Lord

God, let thy promise unto David my father be established: for thou hast made me king over a people like the dust of the earth multitude. Give me now wisdom and knowledge that I may go out and come in before this people: for who can judge this thy people that is so great? And God said to Solomon, Because this was in thine heart, and thou hast not asked riches, wealth, or honour, nor the life of thine enemies, neither yet hast asked long life: but hast asked wisdom and knowledge for thyself, that thou mayest judge my people, over whom I have made thee king: Wisdom and knowledge is granted unto thee: and I will give thee riches, and wealth, and honour, such as none of the kings have had that have been before thee, neither shall there any after thee have the like."

As you can see, Solomon asked God for the one thing that I have found to be the greatest value—wisdom. When I was newly introduced to Jesus Christ as a young child, I repeatedly asked God for wisdom, understanding and knowledge. I would hear my father talk about wisdom when we would have Bible study in our living room. I did not quite understand what wisdom was as a child, but now I understand that it is important to have, and it is needed for every day decisions I make. I have come to appreciate the gift of wisdom.

PRAYER:
Lord, I thank you for giving me the wisdom according to my heart. Lord, help me to use it to your glory.

AFFIRMATION:
I will continue to use the wisdom of God throughout the rest of my life.

BEING WISE IN YOUR DECISION-MAKING

Some of us make bad decisions because we lack wisdom. Some of us make good decisions because we have asked God for knowledge, understanding and wisdom. In Job 34:35, we read, "Job hath spoken without knowledge, and his words were without wisdom." Everyday you will be faced with making a decision, whether it is small or big or right or wrong. Good or bad, words have power, and choices come with a harvest.

Wisdom will help you make the best decisions for yourself, your family and all matters that require a good decision. When you are faced with making difficult decisions, you should let wisdom guide you in a direction of light so that it can produce life. I am sure we have each had the experience of at least once in our lives of making a bad decision. To say we have not would mean we are perfect human beings.

I can recall in my life making several bad decisions. I am reminded that God will let you make your own decision, which is why He gave us the freedom of choosing, "life or death," "blessings or curses" (Deuteronomy 30:19). You have a free will to make choices. I found myself facing major consequences as a result of the decisions I have made. I started to backslide and this also impacted my children, who also began to backslide.

The relationship between me and my daughter was a monster for about four years. Prior to those years, we had a good relationship. Two years ago, God started restoring it, and I was afforded the opportunity to make things right between us. I thank God. She had begun to witness my behavior, which had started to line up with God's will. I had totally surrendered—and changed. I am a woman of God years later, and I am full of laughter, wisdom, faith and endurance.

As you can see, a bad decision can cause the devil to steal the relationship between you and your children. Just remember that the consequences are not going to be fun. As stated before, your children are not exempt from the consequences you may have to face. This is why it is so important to use the wisdom God has given you. If you lack wisdom, just ask God for it. (More information is available in Proverbs 2:6)

PRAYER:
Lord, help me to make good decisions daily. I thank you Lord for letting me learn from the bad decisions that I have made in the past.

AFFIRMATION:
I demand of myself a commitment to make good decisions daily. As I'm reminded of the bad decisions and consequences that I have made, I will latch on to the positive energy and surround myself with positive people and make positive decisions.

USING WISDOM TO RAISE YOUR CHILDREN

Your children are of great value. They are precious to God and should also be precious to you. Your children belong to God. But God gave them to you for a season to be good stewards over. More importantly, you must share with them the importance of giving their life to Christ. Your job is to lead, guide and nurture your children. In a world full of evil and wickedness, it takes wisdom to raise children in the admonition of God.

Wisdom can help you raise your daughters to be modest, virtuous women. It can help you raise your sons to be mature, godly men. Since we were born in a world of sin, we must make sure we do our part to teach our children how to meet the challenges they will face in life.

Your children will respect the wisdom you possess. Wisdom will help you to see their wisdom and allow you to nurture their gift as well as other gifts they might possess. It will also help you to recognize their weaknesses. They cannot identify with weaknesses as children, so they tend to act out in a way that seems right to them. We have all done it before. The ways that appeared right to us led us to a dead-end street. It is your position to teach your children right from wrong so they are capable of making wise decisions in life.

PRAYER:
Lord, I thank you for giving me the wisdom to raise my children

to be well-balanced. I thank you Lord for giving me the wisdom to share with them the importance of gaining a relationship with you our Heavenly Father.

AFFIRMATION:
I demand of myself a commitment to share the wisdom God has given me daily with my children. I will teach them the godly principles so that they can meet the challenges they will someday face themselves.

CHAPTER 12

OVERCOMER

"These things I have spoken unto you, that in me ye might have peace. In the world ye shall have tribulation: but be of good cheer; I have overcome the world."

(John 16:33)

THIS world presents so many challenges. It is indeed an evil world, but yet a good world. The beauty of its nature—humans, water, animals—is so awesome. You have everything you need to overcome the trials and tribulations that come to destroy you, but at the same time build you. You have been made to endure and overcome any obstacles in your path. Just go through the furnace of purification and you will see—"this too shall pass."

YOU CAN OVERCOME ANY OBSTACLE

When Jesus died on Calvary, He had been criticized, used, abused, accused, and tormented. Many obstacles stood in His way such as the Pharisees, the religious minds of the day, as well as Judas and all the hardhearted people. These obstacles helped get Him to the cross. Jesus was full of power and dominion, which was vested in Him by our Heavenly Father. He overcame this evil world: demonic forces—the enemy. Yes, the same enemy we face today. He has equipped us with the same power.

In every area of our lives, we have been given the power to tear down strongholds, cast out devils, and overcome any obstacle standing in the way of our being blessed abundantly. An obstacle is fornication, adultery, lying, stealing, complaining, drunkenness, gossiping—it is anything the enemy has placed in your path to cause you to shift your focus away from obedience, love, truth, faith and fulfilling your ultimate purpose.

The enemy will place obstacles in your path to make you give up. You have had to endure so much because you are broken. You now want to become whole to experience virtue and become the woman you have been purposed to become. These obstacles are standing in your way, preventing you from becoming a virtuous woman.

Can you picture a mountain in your mind? What does it look like? Can you see over this mountain, or is it too high? Say for instance you have to climb this mountain to get to the other side. You have been told that something really extravagant is on the other side of it, and if you can get over there, you will be well pleased with the scenery. Besides, there will be great things when you get on the other side that you will see that will make you want to stay. You really want to see it for yourself. Now since you have pictured this mountain, I am sure you are thinking in your mind, "How am I going to get to the other side of this mountain? It is too high?" Let me ask you a few questions: Are you ready to start climbing it? Are you fearful of the size? In Matthew 17:20 we read, "...If ye have faith as a grain of mustard seed, ye shall say unto this mountain, Remove hence to yonder place, and it shall remove; and nothing shall be impossible unto you."

In this case, we will say this mountain represents all of the issues you currently face, which surrounds your brokenness. These issues make up this big mountain, the obstacles and stumbling blocks that stand in the way of your total freedom. Sometimes it is not easy to climb...sometimes it seems easier to just accept that you are not perfect. None of us are, yet for wholeness we must be willing to be perfected. As this relates to that something in our way, we must develop a desire to overcome to bring honor to God. He will honor us with healing, deliverance and freedom. It is a process, yet if we commit to this process of righteousness as we have done to unrighteous choices in the past, we will taste victory.

As stated before, there have been many women in modern times that have proven through their perseverance and faith that they are overcomers. In the midst of your trials and tribulations you, too, can find confidence in knowing who you really are through your endurance, faith and perseverance.

PRAYER:
Lord, I thank you for giving me the power to overcome any obstacle the enemy has placed in my path. I thank you, Lord, for giving me the peace to know that I am an overcormer no matter how many enemies rise up against me.

AFFIRMATION:
I demand of myself to go through the trials and tribulations, without complaining because I now know I can overcome any obstacle.

OVERCOMING A WEAKNESS

You may be bound right now with a weakness that seems to have control over you. You may not think that you can overcome this weakness. You have come out for a season, but you have found yourself back in the same predicament all over again. Do you know that God loves you, and He wants to make your strength the very weakness that you cannot seem to shake?

God is in the business of using a person's weakness to His glory. He knows exactly what, when, and how to nurture that weakness, and how to give you the power to take authority over it. He knows the motives and intentions of your heart. Tell Him all about your weaknesses, and He will cleanse you and make you whole. You will never find yourself rid of something you felt you would never shake. It has happened for me and many others. It can happen for you!

One thing I now realize is that you have to be willing to change within. You must continue to speak to that weakness. If you are in a certain environment or hanging around certain people that seem to pull you in the direction that captures that weakness, then you need a big shift in associates. You must see associates through God's eyes. You must ask, "Does this person or group help or hinder my progress in gaining healing, deliverance and wholeness?"

You must be willing to do your part, so that God can help you. Granted, it's not always easy, but you must remember what Philippians 4:13 says about your being able to do "All things through Christ..." This, in and of itself, is your power to change.

PRAYER:
Lord, help me to overcome this weakness that I currently have. I know that there is nothing too hard for you. I thank you for seeing my heart. Thank you for loving me more than anyone could ever love me. I thank you for sending people my way to embrace me and encourage me that I can be delivered from this weakness that has controlled my mind.

AFFIRMATION:
I demand of myself to take authority over my mind daily and cast down the imaginations of this weakness that has been controlling me.

A PEAK OF GOD'S GLORY REVEALED TO OVERCOMERS

There is so much glory revealed to those who overcome. God reveals His glory to us during the process of overcoming to help build our faith. Can you begin to comprehend how Jesus felt when He was on His journey for our Heavenly Father? Just think about it! While He was going through trials, enduring hardships, being persecuted, and was literally murdered for the remission of our sins—glory was revealed behind His suffering and His death. He was raised with all power in His hands. The kind of power that no enemy can stand up against!

You can have comfort in knowing that God knows all about your circumstances and is the One who gives you the power to overcome your trials and tribulations—any weakness, addiction. The glory behind your trial—your testimony—will be so awesome.

You will grow to the point of sharing victory (your testimony) and will no longer be reluctant or timid to share. You will no longer be a victim but a victor in this life. You will have a new mind, unspeakable joy, a peace level that cannot be described in words, and infused with the awesome power of God's Holy Spirit. This is your gift for pressing your way through, trusting God, and believing in yourself. You are on the road to becoming a new you—a new creature in Christ who's in the Father. There is no trial that you cannot overcome. Giving your life to the Father through Christ will bring unfold blessings. Sure, there will be trials along the way, but with your new mind, you will see them as opportunities to grow and bring honor and glory to God.

During my many trials and tribulations, I envisioned going to a new level in ministry. The visions and dreams gave me hope in knowing that my circumstances were only preparing me for my purpose. God caused my spiritual gifts to grow with seemingly accelerated passion to do His will. There came a time I could feel my growth with every trial. The harder the trial—the greater my passion became.

The more I became passionate about His will for my life, the more I grew tired of yielding to those dysfunctional, abusive relationships, along with countless other things that I committed and submitted my time, efforts, and energies on. These tempting "things" were not taking me anywhere. They were causing me to lead down a path to destruction. I was "wandering in the wilderness"—the opposite direction of where God was trying to lead me—to freedom and truth—"the promise land," whereby I could be an effective woman and no longer suffer as a broken vessel—continuing to yield to the temptations of this world.

In James 1:12-15 we read, "Blessed is the man that endureth temptation: for when he is tried, he shall receive the crown of life, which the Lord hath promised to them that love him. Let no man say when he is tempted, I am tempted of God: for God cannot be tempted with evil, neither tempteth he any man: But every man is tempted, when he is drawn away of his own lust, and enticed. Then when lust hath conceived, it bringeth forth sin: and sin, when it is finished, bringeth forth death."

PRAYER:

Lord, I thank you for revealing your glory to me. I thank you, Lord, for placing my feet on solid ground. I thank you, Lord, for all of the gifts that you have bestowed upon me.

AFFIRMATION:

I will tell myself daily that I can overcome any obstacle that comes my way.

CHAPTER 13

MEEK

"The meek shall eat and be satisfied: they shall praise the Lord that seek him: your heart shall live forever."

(Psalm 22:26)

THERE are so many things that can hinder us being meek, and our attitude is one of those things. Many people may not know that "attitude determines your altitude." We should take this time to look at the treasures of meekness and the threats to meekness.

TREASURES OF MEEKNESS

A treasure is something that is of such personal high value that any other person, place, or thing cannot replace it. A treasure transcends monetary, market or societal value. For instance, a wedding ring that has been passed down to you for generations might have the monetary or market value of less than $100, yet to you it is worth so much that you would not part with it if someone gave you $1 million. Someone else's opinion or the value they place on this treasure item may mean nothing—it is yours and yours alone. Priceless. Irreplaceable. There can be many treasures. What do you see yourself treasuring the most? Is it your diamond ring your husband bought you for your wedding anniversary? Is it your Mercedes Benz? Is it your house? Is it your 401K? Is it your collection of pearls?

The truth is nothing should be treasured more than your relationship with God. Are you treasuring Him? What can you offer God out of your treasure? He does not need your worldly possessions. Can you offer Him love, praise, joy, meekness, worship, respect, patience, humbleness and obedience? When you ultimately find yourself treasuring your relationship with God, you are setting yourself up for His many blessings.

Here are some of the treasures of meekness:

1. Worship
2. Patience
3. Humbleness
4. Self-control
5. A Bridled (Controlled) Tongue
6. Consideration of Others

WORSHIP

Worship is a form of honoring the Almighty God. Worship also means being in total submission to Him. God loves to be worshipped. When you worship Him that means you are treasuring your relationship with Him, through your spirit. We are spiritual beings. In John 4:24 we read, "God is Spirit, and they that worship Him, must worship Him in spirit and in truth."

Through worship, you show Him how thankful and appreciative you are for His grace and mercy, kindness, blessings, love, goodness, longsuffering, patience, understanding and power. It is your expression that His presence and essence in your life is the foundation for all that you are, and will become. Worship makes the statement that you treasure God above all the material provisions that He has or will make. In Matthew 2:11 we read, "And when they were come into the house, they saw the young child (Jesus) with Mary his mother, and fell down, and worshipped him..."

It does not matter where you worship God. You can worship in your car, on your job, at church, in the closet, in the bathroom or in the kitchen—it does not matter. We owe this to God. If you think about it, when we are in need of a blessing from God, we have no limits as to how, when, and where He blesses us, we're just in a need of a blessing. We say, "Have your way God!" So do not be afraid to raise your hands, pray in your car, talk to God in your car, shout aloud—just reverence

Him.

> *PRAYER:*
> *Lord, I thank you for giving me everything I need to worship you. I owe you worship, so therefore, I can worship you wherever I go.*
>
> *AFFIRMATION:*
> *I will worship God every day. He is so worthy.*

PATIENCE

> *In James 1:4 we read, "But let patience have her perfect work, that ye may be perfect and entirely wanting nothing."*

Patience in essence is saying, "I will wait on God." You can prevent going down the wrong path, the dead end streets, making some of the same mistakes in life when you are patient. It will help you make good decisions. It will also guide you into truth. You have probably been in a situation trying to find the truth about a matter and realized your impatience hindered you from gaining it. Patience is the key to our being quiet and still with the intention to listen for and to God's voice. It's been stated throughout history, "Patience Is Virtue."

Since patience is virtue: Why are so many women impatient? Are you an impatient woman? Do you become distressed or dismayed if you don't see the results you have prayed for fast enough? Are you angry with yourself, others, and God simply because you now face more difficult circumstances, all due to your lack of patience? Let's face it: some of you do not want to wait for a long period of time. I know this because I was one of these people. You would rather do things quick, fast, and in a hurry, instead of waiting on God to do it His way—in His timing.

In order for you to grow in this area, you have to gain the "true lesson" from each test of life, even if it is a test to develop your patience. To pass a test of life, you must be willing to be "patient" enough to hear God's instructions on how to pass it. Mind you, the test can come in any form—anything or anyone who can cause you to fail it by giving up or not standing still—so do not move.

I encourage you to wait until you hear God speak. In Isaiah 40:31 we read, "But they that wait upon the Lord shall renew their strength; they shall mount up with wings as eagles; they shall run and not be weary, and they shall walk, and not faint." Is it not great to receive all the benefits that come with patience? If you have found yourself stepping outside of His timing, and now you are going in a backward motion, maybe you just did not pass the patience test. You did not wait on God. Ask yourself: *Did I get married too fast? Did I buy my house too fast? Did I start having children too fast? Did I overload myself with credit too fast?"* You need to give thought to these kinds of questions. They should compel you to wait, and move according to God's timing and not by your feelings. If you simply wait, you will find yourself passing the patience test.

PRAYER:
Lord, I thank you for teaching me patience. I realize now that I can wait on you Lord.

AFFIRMATION:
I demand of myself to practice patience in my everyday life.

HUMBLENESS

To be humble is to be meek and to be modest. There is always a need to stay humble. Stay humble when you seek God for direction. Stay humble when you are in the midst of a trial. Stay humble when you pray. He hears the prayers of the humble. He can see every tear drop. He can feel every pain. Just humble yourself. Stay in His presence and submit to His will. In Proverbs 16:19 we read, "Better it is to be of an humble spirit with the lowly, than to divide the spoil with the proud."

PRAYER:
Lord, I thank you that I am able to recognize when I am going to a place where I should not be and being reminded that I must humble myself.

AFFIRMATION:
I will humble myself unto the mighty hands of God.

SELF-CONTROL

To have self-control is one of the greatest preventions of yielding to the temptations, the sins of this world—gossiping, worrying, gambling, fornication and adultery. Do not let the temptations control your mind. You need to control the temptations in order for you to gain control over your thoughts. You must have a clear understanding of the liabilities of not being in control. This matter can only be measured by the standards God has established through His Holy Book—the Bible. In 2 Corinthians 10:5 we read, "Casting down imaginations, and every high thing that exalteth itself against the knowledge of God, and bringing into captivity every thought to the obedience of Christ." You need to cast down the imaginations and thoughts that come in your mind to tempt you to partake in actions contrary to the Word of God. Seemingly whatever you think on for a period of time is what you normally act on.

The effects of being controlled by certain thoughts can be very subtle. Any thoughts that are contrary to godly thoughts can affect our mental, emotional, and spiritual health and well-being. Some of us may feel that thinking is of no harm; only acting upon the thoughts is harmful. Have you felt this way? I have. Still, God revealed through Christ that any thought which is contrary to blessings is a curse. In Matthew 5:28 we read, "But I say unto you, that whosoever looketh on a woman to lust after her hath committed adultery with her already in his heart." We must repent for the thought which could ultimately lead to the action if not controlled.

We must not allow certain thoughts to set up camp in our minds.

Whatever stays becomes familiar. Whatever becomes familiar becomes comfortable. Whatever becomes comfortable brings comfort in some way, even if it is the wrong way. By casting down imagination you must destroy the image in your mind. No thought should grow in your mind to become greater than the thoughts that God knows what is best for us—even how to think!

Simply monitor your thoughts. Do not hesitate to attack any thought that is an attack on your peace, joy, strength, faith and obedience in the Lord. When a negative thought arises, replace it immediately with a positive one. You are in control in Christ.

Many of us have found ourselves struggling with self-control in the area of being a good steward of our money. If you find yourself in lack all the time, but you earn enough to take care of yourself and your family's primary needs and much of your wants, then you should do a self-examination to find out whether your spending habits are keeping you in lack.

Instead of allowing your money to control you, control your money by controlling your thoughts. You should prioritize and make God your partner in financial matters. Always sow your money on good ground. Stop sowing on the bad. When God sees you have self-control and you are responsible, He will trust you with more.

> *PRAYER:*
> *Lord, I thank you for teaching me self-control. I thank you Lord that I am able to control the things that have been controlling me.*
>
> *AFFIRMATION:*
> *I decree that I have self-control over anything that seems to have control over me.*

A BRIDELED (CONTROLLED) TONGUE

It is very important to think before you speak. Some of you are not conscious of the choice of words used when you are communicating with others. You will use offensive words and not realize it because your mouth is moving at such a fast rate—you have said it, without giving any thought. Some women just do not know when to stop talking, and I am certain you will offend at least one person a day. In James 3:8 we read, "But the tongue can no man tame; it is an unruly evil, full of deadly poison."

As you can see, we cannot "tame our tongue." Therefore, we need to always think before we speak and make sure we speak positive words—words that produce life. You will bring God honor when you speak words of life. The Proverbs 31 woman opened her mouth with wisdom and out of her mouth she spoke kindness. She was an amicable person. I am certain she knew when to speak and when to bridle {restrain, control} her tongue. Actually, I see this as being a gift. Psalm 39:1 says, "...I will take heed to my ways that I sin not with my tongue: I will keep my mouth with bridle..." Many of us are so talkative. I know it is a blessing to all the people around us when we just say nothing or keep quiet. If you think about it, meditation requires silence. Do you talk more than you meditate? If so, just practice bridling your tongue daily.

PRAYER:
Lord, I thank you for teaching me when to speak and when not to open my mouth. Lord, help me to tame my tongue on a daily basis.

AFFIRMATION:
From now on, I will be swift to hear and slow to speak. I will listen more and more each day.

CONSIDERATION OF OTHERS

To be considerate of others is, in essence, being sensitive. The Proverbs 31 woman stretched out her hands to the poor and the needy. You should always consider others. If Jesus did not consider other people, He would not have fed the five thousand men with the fish and five barley loaves. Jesus did not do this because they gave their lives to the Father through Him. He did it because of their need and Heaven's supernatural supply when we consider others with the mind and heart of God. He can take a little and make it much. (Matthew Chapter 14)

Jesus would not have healed the woman with the issue of blood had he not been considerate. Jesus was considerate of you and me when He healed the woman with the issue of blood whom He had divinely considered. This lady's faith met God's favor in Christ. Her healing was a sign to us of hope and healing. What God did for her out of consideration, He desires for you.

God would not have healed the blind man. This man had been blind from birth. The Disciples thought this man was blind because of sins he or his parents committed. They asked God who sinned. Jesus said, "Neither hath this man sinned nor his parents." He went on to say, "The works of God should be manifested." This man was about to receive a healing from Almighty God. (John Chapter 9)

Also, God's love and consideration raised Lazarus from the dead. He considered everyone, even His enemies. (Matthew Chapter 11)

You should consider your husband and children in the home. You should consider your boss on your job. You should consider your friends and extended family members. Many of you make decisions without considering how this will impact others. When a person is not considerate it can cause some negative impact on the person who is considerate.

PRAYER:
Lord, help me to be considerate of others and help me to avoid making decisions that can potentially impact everyone involved.

AFFIRMATION:
From now on, I will consider others, as I would want to be considered.

THREATS TO MEEKNESS

Here are some threats to meekness:

1. Idolizing
2. Always looking in your past
3. Lack of forgiveness
4. Pride
5. Complaining
6. Gossiping

IDOLIZING

Anytime you idolize a false God, you are out of God's will. Whatever or whoever you find yourself idolizing—whether it is your children, husband, job, car, money, house or any object—you have made that object or person your God. This is definitely a threat to the inheritance that God has promised you. It also makes it harder for you to humble yourselves and submit to God's will—the true living God. In 1 John 5:20-21 we read, "And we know that the son of God is come, and hath given us an understanding that we may know him that is true, and we are in him that is true and even in his son Jesus Christ. This is the true God, and eternal life. Little children keep yourselves from idols—Amen."

PRAYER:
Lord, help me to see when I am putting any object or person before you. I know that you come first in my life and that I should give you all the praise and worship.

AFFIRMATION:
I demand of myself to stay consistent with the Word and only serve the true God—Our Heavenly Father.

ALWAYS LOOKING IN YOUR PAST

Some of you may have found yourselves too often looking into your past. Yes, the past is part of your story, but it is not a part of the new story that God wants to prepare you for. God is concerned with your future. There are lessons that can be learned from your past to help prevent you from repeating the same cycles that you have repeated many times. You must not allow the enemy, others, or yourself, to take you back to relive the guilt, hurt, shame or pain you have experienced. It is the dawn of a new day for you, so embrace it. The Bible tells us the story of how Lott's wife turned into a pillar of salt because He was trying to take her forward, but she was focused on the past. She was looking back to a place of sin, torment and sorrows. (More information is available in Genesis-Chapter 19)

Looking back on your past can hinder you from receiving the many blessings God has in store for you. He wants to prosper you. He wants to turn your past hurts, pains, and disappointments into joy, peace and happiness. He wants to use you so that you can bring Him honor and glory. He will erase your past, so turn it over to Him. In Philippians 3:13-14 we read, "Brethren, I count myself to have apprehended, but this one thing I do, forgetting those things which are behind, and reaching for unto those thing which are before, I press toward the mark for the prize of the high calling of God in Christ Jesus."

> *PRAYER:*
> *Lord, I thank you for delivering me from my past and leading me to a new place—a beautiful and Blessed future. Lord, help me to stay focused on what lies ahead of me.*
>
> *AFFIRMATION:*
> *I decree that I am free from my past. I will continue to press toward the mark in the high calling of Jesus Christ.*

LACK OF FORGIVENESS

In Matthew 6:14-15 we read, "For if ye forgive men their trespasses, your heavenly Father will also forgive you, but if ye forgive not men their trespasses, neither will your Father forgive your trespasses."

Most of us have experienced "something" horrible between our childhood and adulthood. That "something" has caused a seed of unforgiveness to be planted in our heart. You have probably found yourself wrestling with that "something" that deeply scarred you, even to this day. You have been reminded of that "something" that when spoken; it leaves a bitter taste in your mouth. What is that something that has caused you to not forgive?

- Could it have been molestation?
- Could it have been a friend who betrayed you?
- Could it have been an old classmate who constantly criticized you?
- Could it have been a person who fought you?
- Could it have been a father or mother who provoked you and showed favoritism between you and your siblings?
- Could it have been a boss who held back your promotion and/or raise?
- Could it have been a spouse who cheated on you?
- Could it have been someone who accused you falsely?

You should ask yourself, "Am I having a hard time forgiving? Are you finding yourself getting upset about what happened in your past? If so, you need to confront that issue head on and forgive whoever or whatever has caused you to be so bitter. Pray to God, and call out the person by name that may have violated or offended you. Ask God to forgive you and forgive that person(s). You have to release this from your spirit. The Bible says that Peter asked the question, "How oft shall my brother sin against me, and I forgive him? Till seven times?

Jesus saith unto him, I say not unto thee, until seven times, but until seventy times seven. That means 490 times. Who do you know has offended you this number of times? It is now not just the offense that haunts us, it is the fact that we allow the mental pictures of this offense to repeatedly play out in our head. This is unforgiveness that repeatedly shows its' face. It makes us angry beings when we think about it. Forgiveness is not a matter of how you feel, it is a matter of God filling you with the power to release your hurt and release the person who hurt you. You cannot allow this issue to cripple you any longer. It is time to forgive. You've heard the saying, "Let go and let God." (Matthew 18:21-22)

PRAYER:
Lord, help me to release anyone or anything that has been hindering me from moving toward becoming free and experiencing your promises. I thank you for giving me your Word and teaching me how to forgive.

AFFIRMATION:
I demand of myself a commitment to confront any person who I am holding unforgiveness toward in my heart. I will forgive daily anyone who trespasses against me.

PRIDE

Pride is a form of too much faith in ourselves, and our abilities, or any someone else or their abilities, even with worldly possessions. Pride can be a defense mechanism in response to certain injustices committed against us. What I mean by this is that some of us often want to show those who have offended or hurt us that we are "still standing." We are more than they said we would become. We are different than they thought we would become.

We do have to have pride, yet we must look to its source. Godly pride is about God, and because of Him. We have godly pride when we know that in Him we move, live and breathe. We are still standing and pressing on, and more than they said we would become and different than they thought we would become. It is because of our Heavenly Father's love, grace, and mercy. In sum, our pride belongs to God and our pride should be in Him. It is God that we should be most proud of. His pride concerning us is His being well pleased. We have nothing to prove. God is proof!

There have been times when I was in terrible situations, but when I humbled myself, I received His blessings. Some of you are waiting on the manifestation of God, but yet you are lifted up in pride. You have prayed and cried out, but you have failed to realize that pride has been standing in your way. You cannot be lifted up in pride and expect the blessings to come upon you. God does not like a proud look. As a matter of fact, He hates it! When you are lifted up in pride, it impedes the blessings from flowing like a river. In James 4:6 we read, "...God resisteth the proud, but giveth grace unto the humble."

PRAYER:
Lord, teach me how be humble, and show me when I am lifted up in pride. I know that you resist the proud, but give grace to the humble.

AFFIRMATION:
I will walk humbly every day. I will not let pride stand in my way of receiving any blessing that God has for me.

COMPLAINING

Have you ever found yourself drifting into a mode of complaining? If so, what were you complaining about? Could it have been about how much money you were making? How your children were acting? How much weight you have gained? What kind of car you are driving? There are so many things we can find to complain about, but it is not worth it. If we spend as much time thanking God for working it out instead of complaining, we would discover that God is not moved by complaints—He is moved by our faith. In Hebrew 11:6 we read, "But without faith it is impossible to please him: for he that cometh to God must believe that he is and that he is a rewarder of them that diligently seek him." Faith is what turns our situation around. Faith goes out—complaints are internal issues outside of your faith. Faith and complaining are enemies of one another. Replace your complaining with thanksgiving, and you will witness and live the difference.

Many of us have asked God to make us into the woman He has purposed us to be, but we cannot seem to let go of the complaining. The complaining that you have been doing has forced you to come to a stopping point in your life. This is just another stumbling block the enemy has used to stop you from seeing the light of what He is doing in your life. If you think about it, when you complain, it only makes matters worse. In Numbers 11:1-2 we read, "And when the people complained [he's talking about the children of Israel], it displeased the Lord: and the Lord heard it: and his anger was kindled; and the fire of the Lord burnt among them, and consumed them that were in the uttermost parts of the camp. And the people cried unto Moses; [now he's got to intercede for them] and when Moses prayed unto the Lord, the fire was quenched."

Have you ever noticed that when you complained, your situation remained the same, or maybe it became worse? Let me tell you something, you will never get to the solution with complaining. You will never see the light—the change that is about to take place, the freedom you are about to experience, the purpose that is about to be revealed.

Impatience and complaining were two major things that held me back. I had to go through the same tunnel many times before I realized what was really hindering me. You and I have no reason to complain. I thank God that I am free now. I can truly see the light, and I have overcome many obstacles—complaining was just one of them. You can overcome any obstacle, and go from "glory to glory" and "level to level." Stop complaining about your circumstance, just go through it. He has you right where He wants you to be.

PRAYER:
Lord, I thank you for helping me to understand the importance of what you are really doing in my life. I thank you for helping me to see that there is no reason for me to complain.

AFFIRMATION:
I will not complain from this day forward. I will not allow anything, not even complaining stand in the way of where you want to take me.

GOSSIPING

Do you practice gossiping every day? Is it a habit? Has anyone ever caught you gossiping about them? Have you ever caught anyone gossiping about you? Is it easy for you to participate when you hear others gossiping? Do you ever consider how gossiping makes a person feel? Do you want to turn this negative behavior into positive? Do you believe that you are glorifying God when you gossip?

Gossiping is the norm for many women. Yes, this is a real issue at hand that we face daily, and it needs to stop. We need to encourage it each other often to stop gossiping and to be blessing to each other. This is truly an area that most women do not like to admit they have a problem in; instead they justify their negative behavior by simply saying, "I'm just very talkative!" The problem is not being a talkative person. The problem is what you are talking about. Are you saying negative things about people? Why is that? Some of you are always gossiping about others—you discuss what they wear, the way they look, talk, walk, smile, how they live, the mistakes they have made and their faults.

You will go as far as to involve your family, friends, co-workers or anyone who will feed into this negative behavior. When our ear gates are opened to receive gossip, it will release that negative energy that can possibly bring negative problems and circumstances into our own lives.

Gossiping is truly a spiritual growth blocker. What I have learned on my journey is that people who say negative things about others have low self-esteem or they have had it at some point in their life. Some of you really do not feel good about yourselves, unless you are talking about others. If you will search deep within, you will probably find that low self-esteem is embedded there—and it has contributed to all the inner turmoil, which has caused self-rejection. And when you do not accept who you are, it makes it easier to reject others, and gossip about them. When you do this, you are not really for that person; you are showing that you are against them. Brokenness is at the root of low self-esteem and gossip—this compounds so many other things.

I want you to think about the times between your childhood and adulthood when you were talked about. I am sure it has been more than once, right? Now, as you ponder on the negative things that people said about you, I know you are thanking God now that these things do not bother you like they once did. They do not rub you the wrong way anymore. You're free from people and all of their negative opinions. You can care less of how they feel or what they say about you. Even though they slandered your name through gossip, you are no longer affected. Sadly, most of these people were very close to you, right? Well, at least, you thought they were.

Oh, yeah, do not let me forget to mention those church folk. I know some of you have experienced some of them gossiping about you, even now. One of the most amazing things that I have learned about "carnal minded" church folk is that after they have been emotionally thrilled and entertained by the music and pastor's message, they will gather in a circle after church services and talk about you for hours. They will even go home and call each other on the three-way phone call to continue with the gossip. Some of them will even do it in the midst of services. You know the ones that sit on the same pew every Sunday. Sometimes you wonder if they are really there to hear the message. Do you remember the times you walked up on those people who were gossiping about you? Weren't they shocked? And all they could do was offer you a fake smile and hug and say something like, "Be blessed my sister!" You knew that God was moving you beyond what people said about you, so that is why you were (and still are) able to walk in love.

I can remember when I used to gossip, but I had to realize that if I could not say anything to lift people up, then what was it going to profit me to put them down with my mouth. I was compelled to stop after I had become aware of my negative behavior. I had to ask myself: What does it profit me to edify {uplift, encourage} people and tear them down at the same time? Now ask yourself that same question. The Word of God tells us just what we should do regarding this matter. In 1 Thessalonians 5:11, we read, "Wherefore comfort yourselves together, and edify one another, even as also ye do." When you do what scripture encourages, then you will find it much easier to turn negative gossip into positive edification. So when that sister or brother falls short, you won't be so quick to judge and gossip about them, but instead, you will pray and lift them up. Let us stop the gossiping today.

PRAYER:
Lord, I thank you for helping me to speak positive things about others and not continue to yielding to the spirit of gossip. Lord, help me to become more cognizant when I drift in the mode of gossiping, so that I can bridle my tongue immediately.

AFFIRMATION:
I will not gossip from this day forward. I will always say positive things about myself, as well as others, and always encourage and edify them.

CHAPTER 14

ATTENTIVE

"Hear attentively the noise of his voice, and the sound that goeth out of his mouth."

(Job 37:2)

ONE day, I was awakened at 7:45 a.m. by the voice of the Lord. I heard Him say, Ezekiel 36:6. I jumped up, turned in to the Scripture in my Bible and read the word He gave to Ezekiel concerning the land of Israel. I went into a trace when I laid back down to meditate on this passage of Scripture. I could hear every word He spoke to me. *"I delivered you, now you deliver them."* He gave me clear instructions on what to do. After I had received God's instructions, there was a certain peace that came over me. As His voice started to fade, the tears fell down my face onto my pillow, and all I could repeatedly hear was "carry the mantle."

BE ATTENTIVE CONCERNING THE THINGS OF GOD...LISTEN TO HIS VOICE AND FOLLOW HIS INSTRUCTIONS

We are often too busy talking instead of listening. By developing a listening ear, we can gain clarity on what God is saying to us, and where He is leading us rather than telling Him where we desire to be led. Some women have a tendency to think all the time, even when they're sleeping. God is like that roadmap I discussed earlier. He will lead and guide us to where we need to be in life. The only way we can accept His guidance is through listening to what He is telling or instructing us to do.

Do you remember the time you turned a deaf ear to His voice? He was giving you instructions but you had already told yourself you were going to do it your way. God gave Jonah clear instructions to go to Nineveh, but Jonah went to Tarshish instead, fleeing from the presence of the Lord. Well, at least, he thought he did. He caused a great fish to swallow up Jonah for three days and three nights because he disobeyed God's instructions. You see, Jonah had his own agenda. There is no way for you to escape His instructions. (More information is available in the book of Jonah)

Remember, lack of patience deprives us from even taking heed to what He has spoken. And impatience will definitely cause you to hear voices outside of God's voice. Can you think about a time you were so impatient to the point you heard voices (a friend, family member, church member), and you found yourself moving according to those voices, and not God's, all because you were impatient and not listening to Him?

> *PRAYER:*
> *Lord, I thank you for leading my every footstep. Lord, I thank you for being patient with me, although I have not been patient with myself. I thank you for teaching me through my many mistakes. I thank you Lord that I can follow your instructions and not my own. I thank you Lord for giving me a clear Word that I cannot go around your instruction, neither can I escape your chastisement as a result of going in another direction.*
>
> *AFFIRMATION:*
> *I demand of myself to line up with God's Word and follow His instructions daily. I know that I can communicate with Him daily. I will listen to His voice and take heed to where He is leading me. I will speak to Him as He speaks to me. I will walk in His path and not my own, going where I think is better.*

BE ATTENTIVE, NOT A BUSYBODY

Have you ever found yourself not having enough time to communicate with God because you are always on the go? He should be your first priority. You should always find time each day to dedicate your mind, spirit and body to Him. He is worthy of it. Let Him use you the way He wants to. You must understand the enemy desires to take your mind and focus off God. He will find every way to keep you busy so that you will not have time for God.

All of us need quiet time with our Heavenly Father. This time should be used to meditate on the goodness of Him and His glorious works, and to hear and receive His daily instructions for your life. He will show you the plots, plans and attacks the enemy is trying to form against you. Although we know, "no weapon formed against thee shall prosper…" (Isaiah 54:17). Anytime you find yourself being too busy, you need to rearrange your schedule. Do not let the things of this world take you away from the time that is due to God.

There are so many things that can occupy your mind and take up most of your time in a day, such as work, school and looking back on the past or too far into your future. There are a thousand and one thoughts, people, places, and things that can occupy your mind and time. Even going to church too much could steal your one-on-one time with Him. There are churches around the world that have several services per week. Some churches have something going on three, four, five, six, or even seven days a week. There is nothing wrong with going to church. Yes, God gives us pastors after His own heart and churches to fellowship in, and He uses pastors as mouthpieces to help nurture His people, but we must be careful not to turn them into God. We should not we fall in the trap of thinking or believing that being in a building defines who we are in Christ. Who we are in church is who we should be all the time. Not being in church does not mean you are away from God. Yes, there are those who seem to think that if they do not see you in church, you are somewhere doing something you should not be doing. The simple truth to this is Jesus spent more time outside the synagogue (church) than He did inside. The most important thing is your relationship with Him.

What we learn in church or through our private meditations, prayers, and study is to be applied to our life. What we gain in a building should help us to better serve people and God's purpose outside the building. I can remember when I found myself being too busy. I was working a full-time job, being a full-time mother, going to school, and going to church several times a week. My spirit was being feed, but my quiet time with God was being neglected because of constant movement.

The Bible tells us the story of two sisters, Mary and Martha. Martha was troubled and cumbered [burdened] about serving, whereas, Mary chose to sit at Jesus' feet and hear His word. In Luke 10:41-42 we read, "Martha, Martha, thou art careful and troubled about many things: but one thing is needful: and Mary hath chosen that good part, which shall not be taken away from her." As you can see in this story, Martha was quite busy, whereas Mary found time to serve God—standing still. Are you a Mary or a Martha? Have you chosen the good part? Do you like spending time with God?

He loves to be honored and worshiped. There are only 24 hours in a day. You must learn to balance your day, making sure God is getting His time first. Remember, He is the One who gives you the fresh air to breathe daily. God gives you your health and strength! God gives you your eyes to see! He gives you your ears to hear and your feet to walk! He also gives you your mind to think! We must think in a direction of pleasing Him, and not man.

PRAYER:
Lord, I thank you for my having a solid relationship with you. I thank you Lord that it is you who has validated me and not man. I thank you for giving me the comfort of knowing that you are my God and you have sent vessels to deliver your Word, but I am accountable for putting you first on my daily list—first in my life!

AFFIRMATION:
From this day forward, I will give God the time that is due to Him daily. I will put Him first on my list. I am free from being a busybody.

CHAPTER 15

NURTURING

"Her children arise up, and call her blessed: her husband also, and he praiseth her."

(Proverbs 31:28)

WOMEN are nurturers, and this causes us to care more, accept more, and become more attached to people, places and things.

We are very emotional people, yet some of us lack nurturing qualities when it comes to our husband, children, neighbors, and friends.

NURTURING YOUR HUSBAND

Your husband, "the man," is a gift from God. He is anointed by God to lead his home. He definitely needs a helpmate who will not nag him, but instead nurture him. He needs for you to nurture him back into health when he is sick. You should minister to his weakness when your husband is feeling low. You are to help nurture him when he is trying to further his career. You are to replenish him and speak life and faith all times. He needs your prayers, discernment, wisdom, compassion and sensitivity. You husband needs your love. This is why God purposed you as his rib. You have to stay connected to your purpose to stay connected to your husband's purpose. To achieve this, you must stay connected to God.

God created you to help your husband through every situation. You are no longer two individuals; you are now one flesh. You are there to build him up and fill in gaps to make your marriage a full circle—complete—for ministry. The true meaning of the word *ministry* is "service." You must be willing to serve. Service is something you desire to do. It is an honor to serve and you should never feel that service is something done out of your will. You must pray and ask God to help you serve and nurture your husband. "Charity starts at home and spreads abroad," and so does nurturing.

Nurturing does not start with your children. It starts with your husband. It is my belief that God purposed husband and wife to flourish in their relationship and love for one another, prior to having children. The benefits are great when we do things in order according to God's will!

Your children, extended family, neighbors, and all others can be blessed by the nurturing that spills over from the nurturing committed to your husband! Remember, you are God's vessel, filled with love and nurturing, that is purposed for the man of God who is (or should be) your husband. Your service to your husband is your service to the Lord, and all those He has purposed you and your husband to be a blessing to whether directly or indirectly. You do not have to physically serve together in order to serve together as one. You will represent your husband, and you will serve well if you do it the right way.

Once you have committed to nurturing your husband, you should grow in value. His love for you should grow beyond understanding. He should reciprocate your nurturing with his love, affection, protection and always honor you. Your husband should forsake all others for you. This means not only other women who could possibly cause problems beyond infidelity, but anyone who could make you feel second in his life—even his mother. In Genesis 2:24 we read, "Therefore shall a man leave his father and his mother, and shall cleave unto his wife: and they shall be one flesh."

Through my marital experience, I was full of anger prior to my deliverance. I could not possibly have been effective in nurturing my husband in several areas, especially the areas he most needed. The arguing and yelling outweighed the quietness and peace every home needs. A peaceful atmosphere is needed for God to speak and show you all that is needed.

PRAYER:
Lord, I thank you for giving me the wisdom to nurture my hus-

band. I am open to receive any correction and guidance to help me become a better wife.

AFFIRMATION:
I demand of myself a commitment to nurture my husband daily. I will help build him up and support him in everything he does for the glory of God.

NURTURING YOUR CHILDREN

In Ephesians 6:4 we read, "...Bring them up in the nurture and admonition of the Lord."

Women were designed to be nurturers. Because of the adverse effects of brokenness, meeting the mental, emotional and spiritual needs of others is difficult. We are often angry, pessimistic, confused, frustrated, critical and neglectful. Many of us are this way most of the time. We must realize that our children are not responsible for our hurt. They did not ask to be here; they are God's gift to us. We must appreciate the gift and show our appreciation to the Giver.

Our children are precious gifts that must be cherished, loved and nurtured. One of the ways to do this is by being an example of God's love, wisdom, patience and understanding. Our children are ultimately a product of us. They often reflect where we are in our relationship to God. It really is that simple.

Your brokenness in most instances started in the home. Even if your parents were loving and nurturing, the fact that you are still struggling could suggest your parents did not understand how to help you heal. This is true in almost every case. Now in homes where brokenness occurred—whether neglect, verbal abuse or the lack of attention or affection—this often stems from certain brokenness in your mother, father or both parents. Some of us were raised by our grandparents, adoptive parents, foster parents, or guardians and their brokenness could have become the foundation of our own brokenness too. Parents need to know that their brokenness should not continue to be a threat to your child's self-esteem, happiness, dreams, talents and gifts. When our children are wounded, we are wounded. We give our daughters their identities in Christ. We give our sons all of the reasons to love, honor and respect all women and girls, even to respect themselves. You are the first woman your son (s) will ever love, the first your daughter (s) will look up to.

We must be careful not to transfer our brokenness to our innocent children. You must ask yourself, "Did I deserve the treatment that led to negative emotions? Who is responsible for what I have been through? Is it fair to subject my children/child, or my relationship with them to this hurt? Do my children deserve anything less than God's best?"

If you find that your inability to forgive is an issue, you should work to overcome it. Please revisit the section on forgiveness. This and other issues hindering nurturing, peace, patience, gentleness, and "love" must be taken to God in prayer. He will help you move toward understanding and ways to grow in this area. Remember, growing in any area is a process, so be patient with yourself, and you will be surprised at how this will be a plus in the direction of exercising patience with your children.

Always remember that we program our children to respond in a manner consistent with how we approach matters. If we scream, cuss and fuss, then this is what our children will grow accustomed to. Also, there might come a time when they respond in a way which most of us would label as disrespectful. Sure, the Bible states that children should obey their parents, yet it also admonishes that parents should not provoke their children to wrath. If we give love, children will respond in love. If we respect ourselves, our children will respect us. We must always "Give respect to receive respect."

I know from experience that attitudes change for the better when we shift from yelling at our children out of frustration, to speaking to them in a tone of patience and love. Because of the transformation in my life, I have been able to identify just how I programmed the mind of my children to respond in a manner opposite of what I demanded and expected. Things simply do not work this way. To expect to get out of our children that which we did not deposit into them is unwise and is contrary to the Word and nurture of God.

You see, during the various stages leading up to my deliverance I was blessed to identify, understand and address the causes of my issues which concerned my children. My childhood pains, relationship problems, and more were the cause of my anger and impatience. I had to confront head on those issues within myself, and meet the reality of not being who God purposed me to be as a woman and mother. Now I can better nurture my children the way He has intended, and this is true for you.

PRAYER:
Lord, I thank you for giving me peace in knowing that I can nurture my children the way you purpose for me. I thank you, Lord, that I can share with other women the importance of shy they should program their children to only respond to a meek, peaceful voice instead of loudness.

AFFIRMATION:
From now on, I will nurture my children daily with a meek, loving, peaceable, gentle, and kind spirit that is within me.

NURTURING YOUR NEIGHBOR

In Leviticus 19:18 we read, "...Love thy neighbor as thyself..." I can remember being faced with much adversity when I was in the process of losing my apartment. My great next door neighbor was right there for me. She and I talked about the storms we had both experienced and how we made it out just fine. We were able to be sensitive to each other because of our compassion. I was renting some furniture that I had nearly paid off, but my finances did not permit me to pay it off as the storms raged. She purchased new furniture and donated what she had. She encouraged me day after day. She told me to just hold on because my change was definitely coming. She would always leave her door and ears open to me if I needed to talk about anything.

Your neighbor may be beyond the person who lives next door.

Everyone is considered your neighbor. I just want to share this story so that you could understand how we can be a blessing to each other, but it is really much deeper than that. Do you remember me sharing the story about how the Good Samaritan was a blessing to the man who had been stripped by the thieves and left for dead? The Bible gave us this parable to share how we can be a blessing to each other. Again, it was a lawyer that asked Jesus the question, "What should he do to inherit eternal life?" and Jesus responded, "Love your neighbor." (Luke Chapter 10)

PRAYER:
Lord, I thank you for blessing me to be able to nurture my neighbor and receive in return. I thank you Lord that I am open to pray and love my neighbor.

AFFIRMATION:
I will continue to be a friend to my neighbor, and be consistent with the Word of God, as it relates to helping my neighbor.

NURTURING YOUR FRIEND (S)

Have you ever been betrayed by someone who said that they were your friend, but you found out that they were really your foe? How did it make you feel? Did you believe they valued the friendship?

True friends are hard to find, and they are well worth nurturing when you do find them. They need to be brought together by God. Friends need the love, trust and support of each other. To nurture your friends, you must be sensitive to each other's needs. Friends must be able to talk to each other about their weaknesses and strengths. You must show yourself friendly before you can befriend anyone. Proverbs 18:24 says, "A man that hath friends must shew himself friendly: and there is a friend that sticketh closer than a brother."

You can find out if you have a true friend when you are faced with difficulty. Some people are not in your life for the right reasons. They are simply there to subtract something out of your life. We must be very careful to select godly friends because they will be there until the end, and they will add value to your life.

I remember when my friend, Vince, and I first met. He would share stories of how the enemy for many years had him bound. He was open to receive the nurturing and encouragement from me. I emphatically shared with him how God was going to continue to elevate him in his ministry, and He has. The same has applied to all of my friendships. We have all been there for each other. I have come to know that God has to be the foundation of every healthy friendship in order for it to produce good fruit.

PRAYER:
Lord, I thank you for blessing me with true friends I can nurture. I thank you, Lord, that you have shown me how to be a true friend and that you will continue to help me be a blessing to all of my friends.

AFFIRMATION:
I will continue to nurture my friends and show myself friendly.

BONUS NOTE

MONEY AS IT RELATES TO BROKENNESS... CAN IT HELP YOU?

I want to ask you a question, "What can money do for your brokenness?" I know this is an unusual question, but just think about it for a moment. What answer did you come up with? Did I hear you say *NOTHING*? You are right!

Please allow me to share what my thoughts are about money appearing to be a tool to heal your brokenness. You can never use money to purchase spiritual, mental, emotional and social healing. Yes, money can buy you a new house, car, clothes and shoes. You can even go to the spa, nail shop, hair salon, and be made-up to become the most beautiful woman on earth. You can even pay for several cosmetic surgeries, but there is nothing this world can offer you that will fix your brokenness.

We must remember it is not the outside of us that is broken—although it shows on the outside—our brokenness comes from deep within us. I do not care much money you have. You can never pay a physician, pastor or counselor *MONEY* to heal your brokenness. Mind you, you can receive guidance from those mentioned, but make no mistake about it, money cannot do it. Even God does not need your money to heal your brokenness. That alone, should tell you that money doesn't mean anything to God. We are the ones who need money. God has all the riches already. All He needs is your **FAITH**.

You remember when God told the woman that had the issue of blood that her **FAITH** is what made her whole? She had gone to several physicians paying out money, which obviously could not fix her problem.

There are many of us right now who have money to do just about anything we want. We have spent so much money, but we still remain unhappy, and we still have not been healed in many areas of our lives. Many of us still deny the fact that we are broken; instead we force ourselves to deal with our behavior which we believe is acceptable. Are you this person?

Sadly, many women (and even men) have turned to other false remedies—alcohol, drugs, gambling—all kinds of compulsions—hoping these addictions will fix what they have accepted but they are still broken. Now as you can see, money can supply many things, but the real source of healing is the true God. He is the only One who can heal us from our brokenness—in all the areas of our life. God can even shield us from any substance the world has to offer us. As stated before, one thing we must have is **FAITH—RIGHT NOW FAITH.** And we must be willing to admit to ourselves, confess to God and others, that we are broken vessels in need of a healing from Him.

WORDS OF ENCOURAGEMENT

DO not look at where you have been, but continue to press your way to a brighter future, a new level in your life—in every area of your life. You will continue to go higher and higher. Every level you rise to will reflect God's favor on your life and your commitment to grow and "be all you can be." I have stressed this throughout the book: *Do not put any limits on God. He is a "limitless" God.* He can use you right where you are. Do not see yourself as a "nobody" just because you have not met the requirements of man—only God can truly validate you. God has already hired, and is both qualifying and certifying you to fill the position of become a VIRTUOUS WOMAN.

Your application was completed before you were conceived. You are the seed of virtue that was planted at birth. Again, that seed is you—and that seed has been watered with your godly desire for truth, wholeness and freedom. There is no long list of qualifications that you must have like the worldly system requires. The only requirement with His system is that you **BELIEVE** in Jesus Christ, His Son.

It was Jesus who died for the remission of our sins, and it is He who was sent to direct us back to our Heavenly Father. There is no other like Him. He cannot be replaced. There is no stress or pressure of having to study for a test. The test was passed when He went to the cross. Do not worry about the years of experience you must have. Do not worry about what you have done wrong. Just give your life to God—and receive Him in your heart today. And from this day forward decree that you are His daughter, His righteousness, and you are a VIRTUOUS WOMAN of God.

A PRAYER FOR WOMEN

Ladies: I believe that if you say this prayer, you will become closer to God and become one step closer to becoming the Virtuous Woman God intended you to become.

Lord, "this is the day that you have made. We will rejoice and be glad in it." We are creating a full circle of love and compassion for each other. We know that there is power in the prayer of agreement. We will not allow the enemy to keep attacking us in our minds. We will continue to think on godly things and keep our minds focused on you—for we understand that it is not about us—it is all about you, Lord. Father, we can do all things through your Son, Jesus Christ, the anointed One who strengthens us to your glory. We know the enemy does not like unity—we declare that every yolk of division is destroyed through the power that you have given us. We are free and we are overcomers!

*

I pray that each woman who reads this book will continue to strive to become the virtuous woman that God has called you to become. Through all of the trials and tribulations, you can also tell other woman how to stand still and see the salvation of the Lord. The road is not always easy, but challenging times do not last always.

I pray that each woman will instill in her daughter(s) how to be modest and practice virtue at a young age. Oftentimes single women parents use excuses not to teach their children, saying a man is not in the home, but if the woman continues to set the example, the children (boys or girls) will follow.

I pray that each woman will learn to be sensitive to each other's needs. So many of us go through life alone, but we don't have to—let's just reach out and be a blessing to each other.

I pray that each woman will learn to be swift to hear and slow to speak. A lot of us are very talkative. Let us pray to listen more to what God has to say first. We need to listen to our husbands and children. We need to listen to what they say as well as interpret what is said in silence.

I pray that the married women will be good wives and walk in love and agreement with their husbands.

MAY GOD CONTINUE TO BLESS EACH OF YOU ON YOUR JOURNEY OF LIFE AS YOU STRIVE TO BECOME VIRTUOUS

SCRIPTURE READINGS

I have used many Scriptures throughout this book. I encourage each of you to take the time to read them, along with other Scriptures in the King James Version of *The Holy Bible*. Supplement your reading with the New International Version (NIV) of the Bible. I also encourage each of you to read other Christian books written by other male and female authors, new and old. I believe that God will increase your knowledge, understanding, and wisdom.

Hebrews 10:26, 11:1, 11:6, 13:18
Proverbs 2:6, 3:5, 4:5, 6:16-19, 8:11, 12:4,14:1, 18:24, 20:7, 21:19, 22:1, 23:7, 28:18, 29:2, 31:10-31
1 Peter 4:8, 5:8, 5:7
Matthew 2:11, 2:18, 5:44, 6:14-15, 7:16-17, 9:20-22,10:26, 11, 11:29-30, 12:37, 14,16:19, 17:20,18:12-14, 18:18, 18:21, 18:20-22, 21:16, 23:11, 24:12, 26:36-40, 26:41
Psalm 22:26, 23, 33:1, 34:18, 107:43
Jeremiah 1:5, 17:10
2 Timothy 2:15
Isaiah 1:19, 40:31, 54:17
John 1:1-3, 3:16, 4:24, 9, 10:10, 16:33
1 John 1:9, 3:17, 5:20-21
Ephesians 6:1-3, 5:25-29, 6:4
Galatians 5:22-23, 6:2
1 Thessalonians 4:3-5, 5:11
Luke 4:18, 5:18, 6:18, 6:31, 7:6-13, 7:46, 10:30-34, 10:41-42, 23:34
2 Chronicles 1:6-12
James 1:4, 1:12-15, 3:8, 3:11, 4:6, 5:16
Job 34:35, 37:2
Philippians 3:13-14, 4:5, 4:7, 4:13
Leviticus 19:18

1 Samuel 1:12-15, 15:11, 22-24, 3:20, 17
2 Samuel 11, 12:11-12
1 Corinthians 2:9, 3:16, 6:20, 13:1-13
2 Corinthians 10:5
Romans 8:1, 8:5-9
1 Kings 21:5-25
Acts 5:1-10, 10:34, 16:25-26
Genesis 2:24, 12, 19
Exodus 6:6, 20:5
Deuteronomy 26, 28, 30:19
Numbers 11:1-2
Mark 7:6-13

A PERSONAL THANK YOU AND BLESSING TO ALL READERS OF THIS EMPOWERING AND LIFE-CHANGING BOOK

I would like to thank each reader for making the choice to read my book—**From Victim to Virtuous**. My sincerest hope is that you have gained the value and dynamics of virtue and will strive to become the virtuous woman God has called you to become. I pray that you stand strong no matter which trial and tribulation comes your way. Change is not always easy, but through your faith, willingness, confession, meditation and prayer, you can overcome any obstacle that stands in the way of virtue and fulfilling your destiny.

It is time for all of us to take back what the enemy has stolen. God has given each of us power—the power that no enemy in hell or on earth can stand up against. The devil has to bow down every day to our Lord and Savior. Don't look at what you cannot do in the world, because you are a strong vessel spiritually. You are empowered spiritually with the truth to take authority over every enemy for the Glory of God. Your life should glorify God daily.

I also encourage each of you to state at least one prayer and affirmation daily. I believe that once you start to affirm that you are who God says you are, you will see a difference in your life and more healing, deliverance and freedom!

I pray that God will continue to increase you spiritually, mentally, emotionally, socially, physically and financially.

With love, honor and respect,
Yolanda Marshall

ABOUT THE AUTHOR

YOLANDA Marshall, debuting author, was born on August 25, 1973, in Birmingham, Alabama. Ms. Marshall is the sixth of thirteen siblings and the mother of two children ages sixteen and eleven. She holds a Bachelors Degree in Business Administration from Faulkner University in Montgomery, Alabama and a Masters Degree in Public Management from Troy University in Montgomery, Alabama.

From humble yet challenging beginnings marred by poverty and the subtle contractions to Christian upbringing, Ms. Marshall's childhood was fertile ground for the planting of both seeds of blessings and curses, constructive and destructive motives for love, acceptance and happiness. Her family life played roles of both hero and villain.

Recognized for her loving, caring, nurturing, sincere nature even as a small child, falling in love and committing herself to a serious relationship in her teens only seemed natural. Reciprocating her love, attention and affection, something that seemingly had eluded her, she opened herself up to intimacy staking a claim on motherhood, at sixteen years of age.

On her own, living with the baby's father and their daughter, her long awaited haven soon proved to be as turbulent, mentally, emotionally, physically and socially abusive as the world she'd left behind. Transitioning from this relationship to being a young unwed mother on her own would lead to a season in living the party life, another relationship leading to her second child, live in relationship and certain repeated abuses, two failed marriages and more wounds of brokenness.

Crying out to the God of her youth for answers, He would answer and over a period of a few short years would catapult her into the realms of spiritual understanding and move her toward becoming whole. Through a chain of events she crossed paths with those that would be instrumental to her healing and deliverance.

While reflecting on her challenging journey and the many hurtles she'd been blessed to overcome through determination and faith in talking with a dear minister friend, she was infused with a desire to share her story with others, both broken women and girls and the men in their lives. Her life's purpose for the first time was clear, her profound passion to reach out to those mentally, emotionally, physically, even socially broken, divinely revealed: she would author a book detailing her journey through a life of brokenness, repeating many negative life cycles to her discovery, recovering, healing and deliverance—in her first book debut—From Victim to Virtuous.

YOLANDA MARSHALL IS AVAILABLE TO SPEAK AT YOUR ENGAGEMENT (BOOK CLUB MEETING,
CONFERENCE, SEMINAR...)

CONTACT INFORMATION:

YOLANDA MARSHALL
Email: victim2virtuous@gmail.com
www.yolandamarshall.com

FROM VICTIM

TO VIRTUOUS

JOURNAL

*

*

*

*

*

*

*

*

*

*

*

*

*

*

*

*

*

*

*

*

*

*

*

*

*

*

*

*

*

*

*

*

*

*

*

*

*

*

*

*

*

*

*

*

*

www.ingramcontent.com/pod-product-compliance
Lightning Source LLC
Chambersburg PA
CBHW070638160426
43194CB00009B/1500